CALL SIGN -
'ALASKA'

A Survivor's Guide for Flying in Alaska

By

Tony Boyd Priest

CALL SIGN - 'ALASKA'

A Survivor's Guide for Flying in Alaska

©2017 Tony Boyd Priest

First Publication

Published in the United States of America
Published by
ATC Publishing, LLC
P.O. Box 127
Senoia, GA 30276

ISBN-13: 978-0-9910913-8-6
ISBN-10: 0-9910913-8-8

ACKNOWLEDGMENTS

Special thoughts and appreciation for some who lived the Alaskan journey alongside -

Jimmy Gibson, George Jones ("without the guitar"), Jack Hakilla, Michael Hopp, Ed Langdon, Wayne Brockman, 'Wild Bill' Kornell, Michael 'Buck Rogers' Lund, Russell Lash, Ben Jacobs, Bob 'Bear Man' Priewe, Jerry Bagley, Tom Miville, Loren Maack, Dave Rogers, Steve Doty, Roland Suter, Joe Wilbur, Rich Wilbur, Alan Larson, John Robertson, Mark Greig, Keith Washburn, Paul Sentz, George Kobelnyk, Mike Robinson, Tony Walker, Mike Hinds, Bob Penny, Mike O'Neil and Providence Flight Nurses - Karen, Marilyn, Sara, Char, Janet, Margaret, Joni, Kathy and Mike!

I am especially thankful for my Heavenly Father for His guidance, help and protection throughout my life.

PREFACE

About the cover...

The top picture was taken on a bluff overlooking the runway on the remote Island of Attu where air, land and sea battles were fought during World War II. Japan heavily bombed, captured and occupied this Island and others along the southern Aleutian Chain. They were eventually routed by U.S. forces aided by a group of Alaska Native Scouts and sharpshooters donned Castner's Cutthroats.

This was an unusually clear day where you could actually see some of the island. I'd flown down single pilot and after my passengers went about their business, I had time to explore the ghostly hills in the vicinity of the airfield. The terrain is littered with battle remnants of weapons and aircraft.

There were no survivors of the Village of Attu after the war and presently there are no residents living on the island. The photo scene seemed like an opportunistic shot with a World War II Relic against the modern Conquest II.

The lower picture was taken following a winter storm at Merrill Field in Anchorage. Yes, weather can be severe in Anchorage. Best to have your aircraft securely tied down with spoilers on the wings.

About the book...

The book is set up geographically as each type of terrain has its own challenges. The seasons of the occurrences vary.

Incorporated are various Accident Chains followed by notes on how the incidents / accidents could possibly have been prevented.

(As a passenger you may have to wade through some of the aviation jargon on occasion however I believe you'll learn from and appreciate some of the descriptive stories and especially the Golden Rules incorporated toward the end.)

What is an 'Accident Chain'?

In aviation we refer to it as a series of controllable events or decisions that culminate in an accident.

If you closely analyze most aircraft accidents you can see a chain of events or decisions that lead pilots on to the accident.

If you as Pilot in Command recognize a chain of events in progress it's up to you to call it at that point and make a decision to terminate the flight, change a planned route or possibly your destination. Pilot readiness, aircraft condition, weather, airport runway conditions, routing, etc. can all be a part of an accident chain.

Consider this. If an accident is completely avoidable, however wrong decisions have been made leading directly to the accident was it really an unavoidable accident or pilot error? Be aware that several small calculated risks can compound.

All Pilots, Instructors, and their Students need to understand and be aware they may be following an Accident Chain.

As most who've flown with me know I stop everything via my 'Rule of Three'. That is, three elements or factors such as a failed instrument, engine problem, deteriorating weather, etc. added up. Three Strikes. You're Out! It's worked so far. It might work for you.

Whether an aircraft, weather, passenger, cargo or personal health problem, my advice is to be aware of the what-if's and call it a day somewhere along the line. Start over tomorrow with a fresh outlook even if it costs you your job or loss of a customer.

The Accident Chains presented throughout following chapters may reveal a lesson that will help you recognize one of your own controllable links in an ongoing chain.

Having worked for several companies in Alaska which included several years of medevac missions, I managed to experience just about every aspect of flying Alaska has to offer and visited practically every segment of the Great Land.

Sure a lot has changed since the 80's and 90's but I question, with all the technical improvements in aircraft and especially navigation, why hasn't the accident rate improved more? Some reasons of course are the terrain, the long distances, the unpredictable weather, risk management assessments and decision making.

Sometimes those assessments and decisions have to be made in only seconds.

"Experience is like altitude. The more you can draw on the more options you will have to get out of trouble when the time comes. That time will show up, sooner or later, in Alaska."
Tony Boyd Priest

INTRODUCTION

What type of person flies in Alaska with its great distances, unforgiving terrain and unpredictable weather? All types of course.

However, if you're a pilot looking to have a good, long and successful tour in the 'Great Land' here are a few traits, skills and characteristics that will be helpful to you.

He or she...

- Has excellent stick and rudder skills, technical knowledge of the aircraft, weather, and a high level of instrument proficiency.
- Knows the aircraft's and his/her personal limitations.
- Has complete reverence for the scope of the challenges that can appear in front of them.
- Has tons of intestinal fortitude that enables them to meet every challenge with control and a clear state of mind.
- Does not take chances or live on bravado with a giant ego that has no boundaries.
- Knows when to use a calculated risk but always leaves an 'out'.
- Flies like a professional at all times.
- Is not complacent in tasks or travels. In Alaska, Yesterday does not equal today! Change is the constant.
- Is willing to learn from other's experience.

There's been more than 500 pilots killed in Alaska. Most were not flying alone. Related incidents and accidents continue to take lives today!

As it's impossible to see it all and do it all, always be willing to discuss, read or listen to other's experiences. You can learn something from almost any Alaskan pilot who's flown there for a while.

Learning from your own experience is a good thing. However

- Pass... Yes! Experience.

- Fail!... No Experience... Possible Statistic.

So... It seems very beneficial to learn from others experience. Best to get some education before you're tested.

TABLE OF CONTENTS

Chapter One

"I DON'T HAVE ANY FRIENDS THAT ARE PILOTS!"

As summer diminished in 1983, I quickly graduated into my first winter season. I was still with Gordon's Aviation where I had learned a lot about the hazards of flying in Alaska but now I entered an entirely different aspect.

Alaska Aviators had a lot of weather problems early in the winter that year with several accidents throughout the region. Most were fatal. It was during this period we heard the news that a commuter aircraft, a Beechcraft Queen Air, had gone down in the Homer area. There were no survivors.

Moderate icing had been forecast that day with moderate to heavy snow to begin around 10:00 AM.

Somewhere along the line icing evidently became severe causing the aircraft to stall and crash near the airport.

I learned the pilot's names and realized I had seen both at the office just days before but didn't know them personally. I'd assumed they were friends of some of the guys at Gordon's.

That evening, I dropped by the office to check the schedule for the coming week.

Russell Lash, a pilot friend and mentor of mine, was also in the office finishing up some paperwork.

I mentioned, "Russ, did you hear about the Queen Air?"

"Yeah," he responded without looking up shuffling his paperwork.

"I heard they might have gotten into severe icing according to the preliminary report," I continued.

"Weren't they your friends that were in here a couple of days ago?" I questioned.

He looked up, "Tony, I don't have any friends that are pilots."

He picked up his materials and went out the door. I didn't know at the time, but he had given me a strong message. Be careful, and don't get too close to these crazy Alaskan pilots. The mortality rate is way too high. As I found out later, he had lost several comrades during his years in Alaska.

This set the stage for me in the early days of my Alaska career. Russ had unknowingly prepared me somewhat for future events. By the time I left Alaska 11 years later, I'd lost fifteen comrades including two flight nurses. There's possibly more on that list since that time that I don't know about.

I guess it's just a matter of how you view life. As far as I'm concerned there's a strong brotherhood, a bond that grows between comrades in arms or between comrades in any dangerous profession, whether it's firemen, policemen, fishermen, military, or Alaska Aviation. I'd been through a time living with my Brothers in Vietnam. I'd seen a lot of them pass on and had almost been one of them countless times. My take is that I will always feel close to them whether I lost them in combat or in the wilds of Alaska.

Gordon's Aviation to everyone's surprise, closed abruptly in 1984 whereas 25 pilots and flight instructors had to seek work elsewhere.

Many like myself, 'Wild Bill' Kornell and Michael Lund, 'Buck Rogers' continued to fly in Alaska whereas some went south.

Some of the guys went on to the airlines and others went into corporate or air charter. Most of us had various jobs through the years and moved often, making it difficult to stay in touch. Regretfully, several of the original Gordon's Crew are no longer with us.

As typical for the aviation field a lot of pilots lose contact with each other. However, since it's actually a small community we tend to run into each other in the most unlikely places. I've met Alaskan buddies in Tampa Florida and Las Vegas buddies in Ruby Alaska. It's always a refreshing encounter when that happens.

The following Chapters integrate various geographic areas throughout Alaska with accidents, accident chains, incidents, and other aspects of flying in those areas. There's also some interesting Alaskans and other stories presented.

Chapter Two

ANCHORAGE AND VICINITY

Matanuska Susitna Valley

I'll begin here because if you're in the Anchorage area, chances are this will be the direction of your first Alaskan flight. You'll typically launch northwest bound from Merrill Field or Lake Hood located near the International Airport.

Most of the practice areas are out that direction and to get there you have to cross the infamous Knik Arm of the Cook Inlet. It's Glacier fed with ice flows and very cold folks, summer and winter. T.U.C. 3 – 5 minutes. Many have died within a rock's throw of shore.

Elementary to some but good advice for new guys…

#1 Do not begin crossing until you have sufficient altitude to make it to Terra Firma on either side should your engine fail.

#2 Do not cruise slowly and sight see. I recommend travel at the best power setting to attain cruise airspeed and fly directly across.

#3 Be aware continuously of possible traffic conflicts. It can be quite an interesting area as float planes are departing Lake

Hood, crossing at low level, Student pilots in Cessna 152's are climbing for altitude (some have to circle before crossing), and Military aircraft may be departing or on final approach for Elmendorf Air Force Base. Stay vigilant!

You really want head's up in the Pt. McKenzie area just across the Inlet. Aircraft flying in and out of several Anchorage airports converge in a small segment of airspace. Merrill Field has +/- 300 flights daily, Lake Hood almost 200, and Elmendorf about the same.

About Vigilance... I shudder at the thought of being in the same airspace with pilots who've mounted cameras on their glare shields! Very dangerous... Not only that, it seems many do not have cameras focused on the spectacle of the wilderness but on themselves! Continuous Selfies! Where has common sense gone? Believe me. An aircraft can hide in the pyramidal fan of blockage created within +/- half mile of their aircraft. With a closing rate in excess of 220 knots or more and an average reaction time of 10 + seconds there's no time to react. If you're one of those guys this could be your epitaph. "Here lies 'Mr. Smith'... Smashed to smithereens while taking a continuous selfie. Oh yes and there were five others who died in the collision as well.

FAA AC 90-48D talks about Blind Spots and collision avoidance. I'm so particular about that I do not allow a checklist or a chart or any device to be laid on the glare shield! I know many of us teach from our experiences and yes in my early years of instructing I had a close call with an aircraft hiding behind the compass of a Mooney M20 J.

If you must mount cameras please utilize a way to mount and not block your fields of view for oncoming traffic.

Also in your scan be sure to move around on occasion to look up, down and around the normal aircraft structural blockers. If you have something mounted on the glare shield regardless of the hazard, make a point of shifting your viewpoint. Don't totally depend on a technology such as TAS, TCAS, or ADS-B to keep you alive. Any of this can fail you.

Back to crossing the channel.

Here's a consideration - If you should lose an engine or get a rough engine crossing the channel you can stay level of course and let the airspeed bleed off to your best glide speed, or, from that position, announce your intentions and while watching for traffic, smoothly trade excess airspeed for altitude to attain best glide speed. Trading airspeed for a few hundred feet of altitude may give you a better perspective and better view for a landing area especially over water. Why continue at 130 knots in one direction slowly bleeding off airspeed when you don't have a particular landing site visible. Altitude is your friend and as excess airspeed is indifferent to your particular need at the moment best to get up and look around. Just don't forget to capture your best glide speed and monitor it for a few seconds to ensure stabilization at best glide speed.

Wind direction should be a part of your preflight planning for crossing the Arm as well as for performing air work in the practice area.

For instance, if you're not quite half way across but flying at cruise speed, consider the wind direction and consider continuing straight ahead to the other side. Making a 180 degree turn back into your previous tail wind may cost you the edge needed to get to the previous shore.

OK. You've made it across and headed toward the practice areas located around the Mat Su Valley.

As you'll generally encounter flat terrain, your most probable accident situation could be a collision with another training or sightseeing aircraft. Keep good vigilance at all times!

7

For example, training on one clear and sunny day, both the student and I were very diligent in our scans for traffic. It may seem strange but clear blue-sky days in Alaska are the most dangerous in regard to midair collisions.

We were working on ground reference maneuvers and specifically S Turns on a road.

On one of the turns glancing down at the road I saw a converging shadow that wasn't ours. I quickly turned away from the shadow which turned out to be a low wing Cherokee passing slightly above our high wing Cessna. Yes, be aware of shadows.

Following one of the meandering rivers and streams is another way to increase your or your student's stick and rudder skills however use extreme caution when doing so. It's a good plan to survey the river from above to look for any buildings, powerlines or other obstructions along the way and especially be vigilant for float planes taking off, landing or taxiing. If you're in the float plane keep an eye out for the wheels above.

Another hazard of 'clear day' flying anywhere is the attraction of surveilling or photographing Wildlife and with such an abundant variety of Wildlife just across the channel - Tourists pay well to take a tour. Of course, you as the pilot want to provide the best view possible.

Regretfully, many lives have been lost while a distracted pilot maneuvered at low level.

If you're in that situation, #1 Fly the aircraft. Keep one eye on the instruments and be aware of any Airspeed bleed off or uncoordinated flight. Setting flaps at 10 or 15 degrees depending on the aircraft will not only increase your lift capability but will lower your stall speed at the same time. My magic number for most singles was 80 Knots. I made everything else work around that airspeed.

Regardless of the aircraft, choose a safe airspeed with a good margin well above stall.

Stall spin accidents rate up near the very top of the list of fatal accidents in Alaska.

Knik Glacier

Close to Anchorage, this is one of the most popular tourist destinations and one of the most dangerous.

There's been horrendous midair collisions with many lives lost in various positions around this rugged terrain.

The worst midair was further up the mountain over Lake George, a natural lake created by the Colony Glacier. Near the top of the mountain, the lake area is picturesque to say the least and is a popular turnaround point to begin descent down the Knik. The views are simply majestic with the lake and glacier below with snowcapped mountains in your view. However, it's easy to overlook a white aircraft against the snow or to become distracted by the view yourself or your excited passengers. Remember your Pilot duties are #1.

And although you might think you're the only soul within a hundred miles you should always state your position and intent on 122.9 or a designated frequency for that particular area and stay very vigilant.

Other than midair's there's been pilots who were either circling wildlife or had some other distraction and simply flew into the rocks, obviously momentarily forgetting their First Priority – Fly the Aircraft and Always

Leave yourself an 'Out'.

On that note, Your Number 1 Responsibility is to fly the aircraft safely and make solid and correct decisions wherever you fly. The rest – animals, scenic views, passenger requests, comfort or distractions should all fall down the line in priorities. Fly according to your training and maintain your personal disciplines at all times. As a pilot sometimes it's easy to get caught up in the scene unfolding below you especially in the wilds of Alaska.

A 'for instance' for me was one occasion where a huge antlered moose on the edge of a lake was sticking his entire head under water to get the plants below. Now that's something to see - a giant moose with a huge rack doing something weird. Hard to break away… but…do it.

Another occasion flying near Wasilla, I observed a large moose and her calf running at full stride across a large snow-covered field.

I circled back in time to catch a view of a large pack of hungry wolves emerging from the trees in heavy pursuit.

As I observed, both the moose and her calf eventually outran the wolves. I watched the wolves break off their pursuit one by one and slip back into the forest.

I did and there may be an occasion where you have to tear yourself away from a scene like this in Alaska.

You must break your focus on that scene or event and at the very least intermittently clear ahead and around you and check instruments. Be a responsible pilot first.

(That same rule should be in place for conflicting traffic. Once you have the traffic, if not an imminent threat continue to scan the area then come back to that aircraft. Many mid airs have occurred while the pilot was focused on one aircraft and collided with another.)

Getting back to the Knik. There was an incident where a pilot rented one of our Cessna 172 aircraft and with three others aboard found himself out of altitude and turning capabilities while flying directly up the Glacier. He was supposed to have had a checkout prior to flying in that area.

He at least had the presence of mind to make a controlled landing straight ahead. He was quite embarrassed but all walked away. An attempted turn and subsequent stall would have been fatal for all aboard.

The company was able to rescue the pilot and passengers and eventually managed to fly the aircraft off the Glacier.

Climbing up a Glacier is a very dumb thing to attempt. If you're a passenger aboard with a pilot flying up a glacier or a mountainside, and you survive, probably shouldn't fly with that pilot again.

The safest procedure of course is to fly in at altitude and fly down the glacier or mountain side. Always leave yourself an out.

This pilot was obviously a victim of Density Altitude. D.A. is generally not a problem in Alaska, however, lower power aircraft are forever stalling in over 3,000-foot terrain flying over hills and glaciers.

Sneaky, rising terrain can ruin your day. It can be deceiving requiring twice your capability to out climb it. Glaciers are especially deceiving as many times they rise much faster than the surrounding mountainsides.

If you're suddenly over the ice at low level and realize you can't turn left or right, best be looking for a controlled landing spot. It should hurt less than a stall while attempting to turn or out climb the slope.

Here's a sad example of a forced landing north of the Knik Glacier area that should have been survivable. The culprit was simply Density Altitude. The final outcome was due to not following post-crash procedure followed by a simple pilot action. The pilot may have never heard this in a lesson and the subject actually is not evident in aircraft manuals.

An Accident Chain where Density Altitude was a major factor

Link 1 - A Piper Cherokee Archer with two couples aboard, if fueled correctly is generally safe but possibly very <u>close to Gross Weight.</u>

The two couples were on a scenic flight in the vicinity of Independence Mine northwest of Anchorage flying +/- 3,000 ft. MSL. It was a fall day with mostly clear skies.

Link 2 – The Pilot possibly distracted didn't check, ignored or misjudged his Density Altitude and found himself low to the terrain with inability to climb.

In his turnaround attempt he evidently entered a partial stall and contacted hard on the brushy mountain side. If it were a full stall all would have possibly perished immediately.

A fellow was driving up a fire road in his jeep and noticed the aircraft flying low and then observed the entire incident / accident. He immediately grabbed his first aid kit and emergency gear and urgently proceeded on foot about 75 yards up the slope.

Link 3 – Failure to evacuate the aircraft.

When he arrived on the site, he found all were conscious but still sitting in the aircraft. He knew of the possible danger and insisted they exit the aircraft but all refused and asked him to get back to his car and go for help. It was cold and two of the passengers complained of possible back injuries.

He left his emergency gear with them and proceeded to run back down the hill. As he reached his vehicle and put his hand on the door handle, he heard a loud explosion, spun around and observed a huge fireball with the aircraft now completely engulfed in flames.

Link 4 - Speculation of course, but I was told a very important rule long before by a salty mountain pilot in California and subsequently teach it. In the dark, he had me look at the contacts of the master switch when turned on and off. The result was a small arc. Yes the Master Switch can create an arc especially with a load on the circuitry such as radios left on. That spark can ignite volatile 100 Octane fuel fumes. In today's world the culprit could be a Cell Phone that ignited the fumes.

If you're about to have a dead stick or crash landing, just as the checklist says, make sure the aircraft is totally electrically dead before touchdown. If there's not enough time or you missed that check, Leave It On and get everyone away from the aircraft!
This was a tragic loss that should not have happened.

Speaking of Post-Accident Procedure -
A similar post-accident situation was that of a Cessna Caravan which lost an engine just after takeoff from a remote village strip. All survived the glide to a landing but the aircraft had extensive damage.
It was winter and with no time to transmit and no one to communicate with afterward, they settled in for the night. All were huddled inside the aircraft as the temperature plummeted.
With no sign of help and no prospects for several hours the pilot decided to build a fire for warmth near the edge of the crash site.

Regretfully a spark shortly ignited the fuel fumes and the aircraft literally exploded with several passengers inside.

Enough said about fuel fumes and crashed aircraft.

Remember, survival has been predicated on 80% mental and 20 % to all the rest. As most survival manuals tell you #1 Get away from the aircraft. #2 Sit down and Think!

Another Incident -

Two of our helicopter pilots were enroute to Kenai from Merrill Field, lost an engine near the opposite shore of the Cook Inlet from Anchorage and successfully auto rotated to a landing on Terra Firma – a close call indeed.

They had some damage and their radios quickly failed. After about two hours they decided to hike over to Hope, a small mining town just a few miles around the shoreline.

Breaking a cardinal rule, they left the area.

About the same time they were leaving, a search had been initiated by the company.

The helicopter was found in less than an hour. The pilots were missing.

The search continued until darkness set in with no results. The search would continue the next day still with no result.

Well, the haggard, starving pilots finally checked in about 36 hours later in Hope, a very small town on the Cook Inlet shoreline.

They had endured cold, rain, lack of food, dense forest and vegetation, difficult mountainous terrain, and had two Bear encounters. Luckily they had a .44 with them and managed to run the bears off. Although they were both Viet Vets, they were pretty troubled a couple of times and didn't know if they would make it out alive. Hard lesson learned.

McKinley Scenic Air Tour Flights

A few years back on a trip to visit some of my old stomping grounds, I treated my Wife and Brother in Law to a scenic tour of McKinley, now Denali. The aircraft was an older Piper Navajo. The pilot seemed knowledgeable and confident.

It was an unusually clear day for the mountain in November and could have been a wonderful tour.

However, the seemingly competent and very confident pilot began his climb and proceeded toward Mt. McKinley following the terrain flying over and barely clearing the plateaus and the tops of the large rock spires. I was quite concerned and was considering telling the pilot to return to the airport as he was making a 28,000-hour pilot very nervous. However, we made it to 12,000 feet all the while skimming the rocks Upslope.

His airspeed typically was at close to the aircraft's Vy at +/- 120 knots.

Having flown plenty of McKinley tours, I know winds can shift quickly, gusts and downdrafts are to be expected not to even mention an older aircraft's performance capabilities and Density Altitude.

The view at that level was excellent, however for the return, he flew to an open area and descended back toward home base at a high rate of descent. My wife said nothing until we were on the ground but was in great ear pain. She suffered for several days.

This to me is unacceptable. As a passenger on this flight I was Very Disappointed and do not plan to repeat another tour without discussion of the proposed flight with the pilot.

Not only was his technique dangerous, his care for his passengers' comfort was completely absent. Just because a pilot seems confident doesn't necessarily mean that he is experienced or knowledgeable.

A gradual climb to altitude well clear of a glacier or rocks below is a much safer technique. When you arrive at your maximum altitude, you can spend some great time making gradual descending turns on your way down the mountain or down a glacier.

I know I'm beating this one into the ground so to speak. However, the basis is this. Climbing upslope your aircraft's kinetic energy and gravitational potential energy is building but if one is too low to the terrain there may not be enough time to utilize it should something happen. Flying downhill, your gravitational potential and kinetic energies are with you whereas you can more easily get out of a marginal or sometimes deadly situation safely.

Alaska Mountainous Terrain

Keep this in mind as well. Although you follow all the recommended techniques around the mountain, unfelt radical downdrafts can quickly and smoothly bleed off your airspeed. If you're at high altitude possibly in a semi-hypoxic state your judgement could be somewhat impaired as well. For instance, you decide to sneak through a gap on a ridge at a slow airspeed while forgetting to approach the ridge at your 45-degree escape angle. Sounds like an accident chain in progress doesn't it.

Flying around mountain peaks is also a very dangerous proposition. To mess around in a Cessna 150, 172 or most any single normally aspirated non-turbo engine aircraft at 10,000 feet or above is something like Roulette, not something like, It Is. Consider this. If you're in a climbing turn trying to gain altitude to get through a high-altitude pass or across a gap in the mountain, you're probably climbing at the best rate and occasional best angle of climb. What if you suddenly catch a rogue wind shear or turbulence and bump into a stall. Do you know how long it takes to recover a Cessna 150 from a high-altitude stall or spin? What if the wind shifts and you're now on the lee side of a peak and your aircraft's best rate of climb rate is 300 – 500 FPM at best and you're now in a 2000 foot per minute down draft. It can happen folks. Don't do it!

The bottom line and Number one Rule is 'Always Leave Yourself an Out'.

~

OK. You've checked your performance charts carefully and feel there's no problem in pointing your nose up the hill.

Remember, your performance charts and graphs may reflect the numbers when your aircraft was flight tested new and may have been more truthful a few years ago. Most aircraft in the North Country have seen better days long ago. It's not just the engine. Check the leading edges of your prop, wings, stabilizer or elevator. Drag may be quite amplified with chips or dents from gravel, bug strikes in the summer, or simply by the two new antennas.

Another factor is you could lose a magneto or some other engine problem that would rapidly decelerate you and decrease your capability.

Turbulence and downdrafts may occur unexpectedly as well. Both can eat up your planned performance.

A good practice is to get out and perform various maneuvers at planned altitudes and observe the true limits and numbers of your aircraft.

"Knowing the limits of your aircraft's performance is one of several keys to safely and confidently fly a long time in Alaska. Staying alive has a lot to do with career longevity!"

17

If you look at the altitudes, temperatures and Barometric Pressure and the numbers seem somewhat marginal, consider the moisture in the air. What is the temperature dew point? Are there Cumulus clouds in the area? Best to adjust the numbers a click or two downward to be more on the safety side.

Remember, passenger weights tend to be higher in Alaska. Clothing is generally heavier and many will bring everything possible on the flight.

Don't be one of those guys that test the limits continuously. Stay conservative and have a long career.

~

On another note I've run ridges day after day flying the mail in mountains and through passes and felt quite skilled in reading where the best lift and downdrafts would be. Today we have GPS which can read the wind direction and speed and can be a great help in navigating. That's a benefit for sure however, IPads and GPS equipment have been known to fail so be sure to get a good winds-aloft briefing as well as watch cloud movement or direction of blowing snow or dust. Also keep a good old chart handy for backup even if it's expired as the terrain rarely changes.

Best to do some mountain and pass flying with someone who is experienced in that area. May not be an Instructor. Could be someone who lives and flies in and out of the area on a regular basis. Get to know the do's and don'ts before going it alone. At the very least get with your flight instructor for a mountain flying course.

Volcano Tours

Along the Cook Inlet, sometimes referred to as the 'Volcano Coast' and in scenic flight range of Anchorage are several active volcanoes. Mt. Spurr sits off to the west and across the inlet. Further south is Mt. Redoubt and Mt. Iliamna volcanoes. Augustine volcano sits in the water west of Homer and Anchor point.

That's great of course for tourists and scientific types however on occasion they become a real problem for aviation.

For example, another one of our Cessna 172's flying toward Talkeetna came back with an opaque windshield and well sanded leading edges after encountering a fine grain ash falling from what seemed like blue skies.

Luckily the air filter held up as he worked with ATC to get back to Anchorage. On arrival, he then side slipped the last few miles to finally land on the large runway at Anchorage International. He was lucky to make it back.

When planning a flight around Anchorage or the Kenai Peninsula it's a good idea to include a look at Mount Augustine, Mount Redoubt and Mount Spur for activity and to check winds aloft for direction of any plumes.

All have a history of sudden and un-forecast eruptions leaving heavy accumulations of volcanic dust on the ground at Anchorage, Kenai or Homer. Some of the plumes of ash can stretch as far away as Canada and the Yukon Territory.

There are several examples of situations including Airline operations described in my previous book Call Sign Iceman. I personally had two very close calls at Mt. Spurr and Mt. Augustine.

Mt Redoubt erupted drastically in 1989 and covered Anchorage in ash. About a week later I ended up with a dead stick landing with a student in a Cessna 152. We were returning from a short cross country flight and encountered a rough engine situation. I tried every means possible to keep it flying but soon realized we were not going to make the airport.

I'd identified an old short gravel strip and had remained in gliding distance just in case. And... as the engine quit for the third time, "That's it." I pulled the mixture and set up for a landing.

The landing was successful and being on the outskirts of Anchorage and with a short walk down the road made it to a phone. We were picked up shortly thereafter.

Later the mechanics made it to the airstrip, spent a couple of hours and flew the aircraft on over to Merrill Field.

They reportedly found ash 'mud' in the carburetor and fuel filter. Back at home they drained the tanks, washed them out and put fresh fuel aboard.

Use caution anytime you fly with 'any' quantity of ash drifting down or blowing around on the ground.

Okay. Now to get out of the Anchorage 'Bowl' Area...

Chapter Three

FLYING ALASKAN PASSES

Many of the surrounding mountain ranges generally require you to fly the passes or fly completely around the mountains. Large stretches of several mountain ranges are simply too high to navigate across for most aircraft. Jets or pressurized turboprops are your best bet but most are not flying those.

Flying these pristine wilderness passes through the rugged Alaska terrain can be the most exhilarating and rewarding flying there is. However, when there's cloud cover with freezing levels lower than surrounding peaks, passes are a necessary route of travel.

Flying a pass under those conditions can be extremely hazardous.

In Alaska I've found unexpected precipitation the primary weather hazard as it can lower the ceiling and visibility at a dramatic rate. Next are the other dangers, wind creating severe turbulence, up and down drafts and density altitude.

Alaskan pass elevations are generally lower than most Rocky Mountain passes which seems somewhat strange as several Alaskan mountain ranges have peaks much higher than you find anywhere in the lower 48.

There are a lot of good books out there on mountain and pass flying, so I don't plan on re-writing what's already written. If you haven't read them, please do so before you go north. If you fly airplanes, read them anyway.

I've included this chapter to share some of my personal experiences through the years. Before you take on pass flying ensure that you know your aircraft's limitations very well and that your stick and rudder skills are sharp. For initial pass flying consider taking along a flight instructor or someone who has experience there.

The concern is that even a seasoned pilot can get into trouble very quickly in any mountain pass. Alaska passes can sometimes be extremely dangerous with the rapidly changing weather.

I recommend you take a careful look at all aspects of each pass you intend to fly. Utilize a sectional chart and lightly circle prominent landmarks as well as note what your personal minimums should be. In the straighter parts draw a line and plot your magnetic courses along that line. That will enable you to ensure you're in the right canyon or valley. Fly with the folded chart on your lap and have a planned 'out' for each section of the pass.

After being caught a couple of times thinking I was comfortable with a two-thousand-foot ceiling, I raised my personal ceiling minimum to three thousand feet. Ten miles visibility is a pretty good number. Just be aware of possible precipitation.

My minimums were generally higher than most simply due to several close calls encountered. A 'close call' becomes experience when you survive. You can become a statistic when you don't. With well over 10,000 hours in practically every nook and cranny in Alaska I suggest it's best to fly in a conservative manner.

I placed another limitation on myself for pass flying or for scenic tours around mountainous terrain. That was a winds-aloft forecast of 25 knots anywhere close to my planned altitude. 25 knots are bad enough but with the acceleration factor of the wind passing over ridges, peaks or through narrow adjoining canyons it can really get rough. Up and down drafts along with occasional invisible rotors become the norm and are quite hazardous to your health. Occasionally a severe downdraft can be smooth as well and if maintaining level flight with a visible horizon or while on auto pilot it's easy to allow your airspeed to 'bleed off'. A spot check of your instruments is important especially your airspeed and current heading.

Another area where conditions can surprise you especially in the evenings is in a pass where glaciers spill into it. The phenomenon is typically a downslope wind condition called 'Mountain Breeze' where winds flow down the glacier. 'Valley Breeze' where winds can pick up moving up the glacier during the day may not be so prevalent. All depends on the size of the glacier. Either can be detrimental to your flight condition. Keep an eye on your airspeed traveling by those beautiful rivers of ice.

If at all possible, utilize proper pass flying techniques and travel along the right side if able. For example, flying down the middle of a pass you've limited your turn around radius should you encounter deteriorating weather. Flight along the left side to be in smooth air can be hazardous as you may have opposite direction traffic in that area. However, on occasion it may be necessary to fly there to avoid turbulence or downdrafts on either side however one needs to be constantly vigilant. It's not a good place to meet an old buddy.

Never ever scud run in a pass. Even if you've been through several times terrain can be very deceiving especially when there's low visibility or showers. Fog and haze have a way of distorting the terrain.

Also in pass flying be very aware that it's easy to become distracted from your primary duty to Fly the Aircraft and Avoid Terrain!

If you have an opportunity to discuss pass flying incidents with other pilots or attend a safety seminar, you'll discover that even with proper planning and techniques there can be problems. Accidents in mountain passes are usually fatal.

Unexpected precipitation incident - Proceeding through a nice wide pass with a 5000-foot ceiling in our Cessna 310R – Day / VFR…

All was normal when suddenly snow began to fall. Visibility began to drop and my ceiling rapidly began to lower. One minute ago I could see 20 miles. I immediately banked slightly left to look behind and realized there was nothing at all to see now except white. Looking back ahead I began losing the terrain. I suddenly could see nothing except heavy white snowflakes on the windshield!

I knew where I was and my 'pass cardinal heading' for my current location at the time. I didn't hesitate and zoom climbed on my heading straight down the center of the pass.

As I cleared the highest obstacle in the area, I contacted ATC and filed IFR on to my destination. Notice the priority. Fly – Navigate – then Communicate. There's no reason to attempt to call anyone when you're below the walls of a canyon. They cannot help you in any way! You Are 911!

An example of another timely action was on a medevac flight enroute to Seward. We had a very critical patient there which really concerned our somewhat frantic nurses.

Approach minimums are quite high there and as usual Seward was below the ceiling minimums.

Conditions there were VFR with winds calm and visibility more than 10 miles below an 1800 ft. ceiling.

We had a very capable IFR Known Ice aircraft but with stubborn weather below IFR minimums we contemplated our options and decided to head down VFR low level through the mountains. We both knew the passes very well.

We selected our best route and decided to fly to Skilak Lake and then navigate the mountains eastward to Seward.

Entering the mountains, we proceeded along easily for a time however we knew nearing Seward there was a 'bend in the road' and it would be coming up shortly. Our out was an area where two passes connected. It was a wide area we could utilize if necessary for a turnaround. We discussed this point as our last 'Out'.

As we approached the bend, we slowed to 100 KTS and applied approach flaps in advance just in case the pass into Seward was blocked.

We were prepared and sure enough as we hugged the right-side rock wall and came around the bend there was a wall of white ahead.

We utilized an immediate 45-degree bank angle turn, completed our 180 and remained clear of the wall of fog and the rock walls. (I'll review the complete technique we utilized at the end of the chapter.)

As you can imagine, when a pass has turns left and right with high rock walls everywhere it's not a good idea to attempt a Chandelle or even a zoom climb as you might be flying directly into the rocks.

That fatal scenario has happened all over Alaska!

During our turn around we had a couple of screams from the Flight Nurses who settled down when they realized we were stable and in clear air headed home.

25

Although I've transitioned through just about every pass in Alaska at some point I'm only including a few whereas most of the lessons can apply to pass flying throughout the Great Land. The following passes discussed will include some actual experiences and details of the terrain.

Portage Pass ('Red Pin')

There's been others but my closest call was the one in Portage where I became trapped over Portage Lake. If you'd like to revisit that one it's in Chapter 31 - Call Sign 'Iceman'. It was a very narrow escape.

Why 'Red Pin' you ask?

Call Search and Rescue at Elmendorf AFB and possibly get permission to stop in for a visit.

Our company was involved in a coordinated search for an overdue aircraft and in conjunction we were invited to view their search map.

Their large wall map of Alaska was dotted with hundreds of red pins.

I immediately asked, "What is that!" looking at a small mountain of red pins.

"That's Portage Pass area. We no longer mark the new ones because there's so many. As you can tell we could have a real problem locating a current crash site in that area."

After that discussion I nicknamed Portage Pass 'Red Pin' Pass'.

Enough said.

I'm sure they're on a digital map system these days however should still be quite interesting.

Located between Anchorage and Whittier on the Prince William Sound, it's one of the few passes you can drive through in a manner of speaking. In your car you get to share a 2.5 mile rail road tunnel with the train. It's a 'trip' you should experience at least once. Well that means twice because you have to come back through the tunnel as the last road dead ends at the end of a concrete dock adjacent to the Prince Williams Sound!

Kind'a funny note... One absolutely beautiful, smooth blue-sky day enroute to Cordova we were transitioning VFR through the pass with our Beech 99 and about 10 passengers.

Being the greatest scenic tour pilot in Alaska, I was making gentle turns and pointing out specific scenic points along the way.

When after about 10 minutes, the co-pilot tapped me on the shoulder and motioned for me to look back.

Yes. Every passenger was sound asleep. Locals....

It is one of the most beautiful passes in the world and when you break out of the pass over the small town of Whittier, you're looking at the bluest of blue water with scattered white capped mountains and glaciers.

A word of caution – Should you lose an engine along the Turnagain Arm enroute to Portage Pass, do all you can to put the aircraft down on the road or near to the road. I do not recommend putting it down on the mud flats. Looks very inviting, however... That beautiful flat area can become quicksand in an instant depending on the Tidal Actions. With the unpredictable glacial silt, you may be landing on concrete or on quicksand. If you end up somewhat away from the shoreline you might consider remaining on top of the wing until help arrives. I've observed the very fast moving 'Boar Tide' from aloft many times sweeping into the Arm with a large standing wave leading the way.

Regretfully there are horror stories where lives were lost along that pristine shore. You can look up the Adeana Dickinson article 7/16/88 which occurred during my time in Alaska.

Lake Clark Pass

With the exception of a couple of weeks passing by a Cherokee Arrow stuck in a glacier near the pass entrance I've enjoyed traveling through this one. The pass is long, wide, scenic and pristine. At moderate altitudes there's plenty of room to maneuver and enjoy the many glaciers and waterfalls surrounded by snowcapped mountains and radical terrain.

From over the south Cook Inlet you make a turn to the Southwest to enter the pass. After an enjoyable journey, it opens up to Lake Clark, a clear and pristine glacier fed lake. Great Fishing!

The airport there is great and the folks very hospitable.

Following the river at lower altitudes in good conditions can be quite enjoyable as well. The snow on the glaciers seemingly billows out of the rocks on both sides.

The fatal accident referred to earlier was that of a Piper Cherokee Arrow with four aboard which crashed near the top of a steep glacier.

A combination of weather and terrain may have caused the pilot to fly directly into the glacier near the top of the mountain.

What a macabre feeling to fly by that aircraft day after day with the people still sitting in it. The nose and most of one wing was not visible. The unreal scene was that of a dart stuck in the mountain. Search and Rescue had verified all were killed but were forced to abandon the retrieval due to altitude and poor weather conditions. The bodies were finally retrieved however the aircraft remains a part of the glacier.

The speculative cause was with the weather marginal at best, the pilot was attempting to enter the pass and in the poor visibility thought a light area in the clouds was an opening. As mentioned earlier in 'Call Sign Iceman' a glacier may reflect sunlight in broken clouds or marginal visibility and can be quite deceptive.

A similar accident following a long 'Chain of Events' is described in detail in the coming chapter 'Break the Chain!'

Always review your chart for the highest terrain plus obstacles within 10 miles of your route and plan your 'out' accordingly.

Statistically two thirds of the accidents caused by 'continued VFR flight in reduced visual references' are fatal. Why would you risk it?

Rainy Pass

Rainy is the shortest route to Nikolai and several Kuskokwim villages. Its main claim to fame is that the famous Iditarod Trail follows the route. Very famous of course, well-traveled, but can be extremely treacherous. There are many twists and turns 30 – 50 degrees with a couple requiring up to 90 degrees of turn. As you proceed through there's generally rocks on all sides and areas where right or left choices have to be made.

Study your charts extremely well and note any particular geographic points. Best to have this one really lined out on your sectional with landmarks, turns to headings and distances showing.

I do not recommend this pass in precipitation or with ceilings in the pass below 2,000 feet.

Ptarmigan

Crossing the Alaska Range – Rainy VS Ptarmigan

A few of you that have read Call Sign Iceman know what the 'VS' is about. You know what I'm going to say about it and already know some of the lessons I'm trying to instill in new guys. Alaska flying is all about making decisions. Making the right choice at the right time comes with experience. Sometimes you have a few hours to plan, sometimes a few minutes, sometimes only a few seconds. There are however, occasional times where the door behind slams shut and you may be totally relying on your skill and experience to stay alive.

'Here was yet another day when I was following my friend, Wayne Brockman and flying second section to Fight 501 headed to McGrath, Alaska. The ceiling was 3,000 feet with visibility better than 10 miles. I remained in trail of Wayne as we crossed the Cook Inlet Basin and entered the mountains. We were planning on transitioning the Alaska Range via Rainy Pass, which would get us over in the least amount of time.

As we approached the 90 degree turnoff point leading into Rainy Pass, it began to snow.

"Wayne, how's it looking up ahead?" I asked.

"Well, it's not looking real good, light snow, but not looking that bad either," he replied.

"Better take a good look before you go into Rainy," I suggested.

"You're right about that!" he replied.

Both he and I had flown through the pass many times and knew it quite well. The worst part consisted of a couple of turns around snow covered peaks. That's not bad on a clear day, but it was overcast with a good chance of whiteout should it begin to snow heavier.

30

"Yeah, Tony, I think I'll take a look. I'll let you know how it is," he said. Wayne made his turn into the pass and a minute later, I was approaching the entrance also. Suddenly, the snow showers picked up in intensity and the pass entrance began to disappear.

I keyed the mike, "Wayne, it's starting to snow pretty hard out here, how's it look?"

"Well, I don't know. It's snowing harder in here also," he answered.

After a brief pause, "Gettin' pretty bad now...Snowing heavier...Gettin' into white out condi..."

"Wayne, say again. You're breaking up. Can you turn around? Wayne..."

At that point, I lost contact with Wayne. I was worried of course as it was snowing very hard now. Visibility had dropped to the point that I could not identify any landmarks looking into the pass entrance.

I took my planned out at this point, banked left and headed toward the nice and wide Ptarmigan Pass. Ptarmigan branches off from that part of Rainy, goes 25 miles south and then opens out to the west and into the Kuskokwim valley. The feeling is something like you feel turning off a twisting secondary road and jumping on the freeway. We both were low in the mountains and I knew radio reception wasn't that great anyway. However, I had a gnawing feeling going on and continued to attempt contact by every means possible for the next 30 minutes.

As I flew out of Ptarmigan and into the tundra area, I called Nikolai, the closest village. With no answer, a few minutes later, I radioed McGrath Flight Service and began a communication search for the missing plane. I was feeling quite anxious at this point.

31

Suddenly I heard a scratchy radio signal, "…Six Juliet Whisky departing Runway… Nikolai…"

I gave him a minute. "Wayne, are you up?"

"Hey, Tony, what's going on?" he said.

"Wayne, how are things? We've been looking for you," I said.

"Sorry 'bout that. Came out of the pass pretty low, went straight over to Nikolai and dropped off the mail. It got pretty tight in the pass there. I always had ground contact, but it sure was snowing. Let's have a coffee in McGrath."

"Sounds great Wayne. How far you out?" I responded.

"Looks like about 11 minutes… see you there." he answered.

As I glanced at my DME, 13 minutes! 'Doggone, he's going to beat me to McGrath…again!'

I was quite relieved of course but concerned at how a seasoned pilot could get into trouble in a couple of minutes in a mountain pass. The answer of course is the forever changing weather.

Over coffee, Wayne seemed cool and collected, but after discussion, we both had raised our personal minimums for Rainy Pass.

Mountain passes can be dangerous no matter where they are. Alaskan passes can be extremely hazardous. I was just glad to have my good friend one more day.' (Excerpt from Call Sign – Iceman).

The Ptarmigan Pass route is about 25 miles further but should be considered with precipitation or per the area forecast.

Merrill Pass

This is a short pass but can be challenging with several lookalike gaps in the mountains. There are many relics of crashed aircraft on the steep mountainsides.

32

It's a different pass in every season. When all is snow covered it's quite hazardous and easy to make a wrong turn especially in marginal visibility. There are high mountain peaks and lots of adjacent vertical rock spires in the vicinity.

Best to fly through this and all passes you intend to fly with an experienced instructor more than once in winter and in summer.

That's it for now but please be sure to do your homework before any pass flying.

Alaska's unpredictability may dictate unusual action

Speaking of passes, there may be times when you're suddenly confronted with a wall of weather or lowering ceilings.

Much of the summer months carry a low overcast with fairly good visibility below. However. that's when most are flying.

My personal pass ceiling limits varied depending on the terrain geographical features of that pass.

Be sure to set your ceiling limits early and stick to them! Don't adjust as the mission dictates. Find another route.

Only adjust personal limits as your proficiency dictates! Stick to your Limits, Fly a long time!

Iceman Blind Canyon Turnaround (The Maneuver)

The Blind Canyon Turnaround, after careful analysis and practice, is a maneuver I developed during the late 70's. It was designed to get me and my guys out of trouble when encountering sudden loss of visibility in canyon situations.

I began looking for alternatives to the Chandelle following an accident in California where the pilot tried to execute a Chandelle Maneuver and contacted the canyon wall about 2/3's around his turn. There were four fatals in that case and many more reported through the years.

I've heard other methods discussed such as a Hammer Head to reverse course, although I've not met anyone who performed a Hammer Head 'turnaround' in actual conditions.

Another pilot I discussed the situation with had executed a spin to get below a rapidly dropping ceiling and actually survived. (He's the same one that 'bumped-jumped his aircraft over a frozen bull dozer parked in the middle of a one-way mountain mining strip and survived. Evidently quite a skilled pilot. Not so sure of his techniques.)

I wouldn't recommend any of those maneuvers.

Of course, follow all the canyon and mountain flying rules to stay alive, but maybe take a look at a maneuver that demonstrates your aircraft's maximum 180-degree turnaround capability while keeping your present altitude constant and your turn within the smallest radius possible. The maneuver only applies to aircraft with Slotted or Fowler type flaps which produce lift. I have not attempted the turn around with Plain or Split flaps.

Here's the maneuver to practice. All aspects remain within the aircraft's normal parameters of operation however I recommend you have a Commercial - Instrument Rating, be proficient on instruments and have sharp stick and rudder skills.

To set up the maneuver ensure you're at least 1,500 feet AGL as required and for your first attempt and practice use 2,500 or 3,000 feet. Clear the area and announce your intention. A straight vacant road or roadway close to your left side is best to start with. Power should be at a low cruise setting just as you would when weaving through a curvy pass. Of course, if you're on a straight pass with decent visibility normal power settings are fine.

Your goal is to complete a 180-degree turnaround with no loss of altitude and to arrive over or close to the road.

First, find or visualize a landmark to represent a 'wall' ahead. Then reduce power to idle and bank forty-five degrees left or right depending on where you are. Maintain exact altitude. Select full flaps if electric or manual flaps to full in increments at the soonest possible moment as speed limitations allow. Maintain Altitude. As your speed decreases to Vy (due to idle engine power and your bank angle) introduce full Throttle. (This should occur at approximately 90 degrees into the turn.) Then begin rolling out of your 45-degree angle of bank as you're attaining your 180-degree exit heading. Reduce flaps as your airspeed again builds and maintain your one hundred eighty-degree reciprocal course.

Detailed Description: (Be Precise**)

1. Quickly reduce power to Idle. (Carb heat first if in normally aspirated engine.) By doing this you will decelerate at a rapid

35

rate. Hold your altitude. This will require some back pressure and trim in most aircraft. (3 to 5 seconds)

2. Bank 45 degrees left or right depending on where you are of course. Maintain no more or less than 45 degrees for as you know stall speed increases with bank angle. Add Power as required to maintain **Vy** as your minimum airspeed during the maneuver.

3. Select Full Flaps if Electric as they extend slowly enough to remain in limitations. However, monitor your specific aircraft Flap numbers so as not to over stress. Extend Flaps in increments if Manual at the top of every speed available.

4. Then at approximately 90 degrees into the turn approaching Vy, increase to Full Power or enough power to maintain Vy. Keep your Vy airspeed constant.

5. Approximately 135 degrees begin Roll out and reduce Flaps as you continue to roll out on your 180-degree track. Adjust your power setting as you reduce flaps and accelerate to your normal pass speed. The balance between Flaps / Bank / Power vs. Stall Speed can be held quite nicely during the entire maneuver.

I've used this maneuver several times in various aircraft and in actual situations.

*Chandelle – Radius of turn is too large plus you don't want to climb into a ceiling as passes typically are not straight and have rock protrusions.

**Be precise. Altitude within 50 feet. Airspeed (Vy). Flap speeds within 5 knots. Bank Angle 45 degrees with 0 Deviation! (More than that you begin creating excessive G force (Load Factor) increasing stall speed and safety margins plus you may tumble gyros!)

Chapter Four

NORTHERN ALASKA 'OUTBACK'

Once slipping through the Alaskan Range and following the Kuskokwim or 'Kusko' as the locals call it there were several memorable occasions that left impressions worth mentioning here. Many destinations such as Fairbanks, Bethel, etc are not mentioned as things are more standardized. I'm hoping you will pick up some helpful items from several short stories regarding the more remote villages and airfields.

Always call first to make sure your landing there is okay and to check for visuals on current weather and landing conditions.

Also it's a good practice for any pilot traveling out to this wilderness country, along with adequate survival supplies and tools, to keep a list of the "Dry" Villages in your flight bag or at least have access to it.

If you suspect that alcohol is concealed in boxes or bags of your passenger's baggage or cargo headed to a dry village, confront that person or possibly contact someone in management or law enforcement. Don't chance losing an aircraft to the state or winding up in jail by unknowingly transporting alcohol to a dry village!

Farewell (FWL)

Located about 150 miles from Anchorage lies the now abandoned 'town' of Farewell. I flew in there on occasion usually with Government Types aboard.

The Caretaker / Manager at the time lived quite alone and was an interesting individual. During the 80's and early 90's there were several buildings located near the airstrip.

One sunny spring day I had six folks aboard my Conquest II, four men and two ladies, government but not sure what branch as most tended to not share missions.

The landing was fairly normal with the exception of rough runway conditions which included some right and left movements to avoid large rocks on the runway.

As the engines shut down the defining silence of such a dramatic setting hit everyone as they stepped onto the graveled ramp area.

The adjacent mountains were tall granite spires that shot up into the azure blue sky.

After distributing their brief cases and small bags, we all proceeded toward one of the buildings.

There were no vehicles around and the place seemed totally deserted.

Suddenly a door opened on one of the rustic buildings and a large fellow wearing overalls and half tucked in shirt appeared. Unshaven and with a partial beard he wasn't a pretty picture.

However, we were greeted warmly and offered some coffee or tea.

The passengers seemed more anxious to get to their undisclosed tasks and went their separate ways.

After completing my post flight inspection, I took him up on the coffee and spent some time talking about his life and how he ended up as the sole resident of Farewell Alaska.

As things progressed it seems he had some animals including two cows. That was strange in itself as to how he managed to get two cows to such a remote place. It seems there may have been a circumstance where a Cargo Carrier with an engine problem decided to leave them there.

However he sadly explained that a large Grizzly had torn the door off his barn, killed his favorite cow and ran off with most of the carcass.

I later learned his name was 'Bill' and found his stories quite interesting. I later learned he was a Vet and in Vietnam about the same time and in the same area that I was.

We traded a few stories and shared some soup he'd put together for lunch.

As the folks began to return I left and began my preflight duties and prepared for the flight home.

The caretaker walked the ladies to the aircraft and all said their goodbyes.

I thanked him for his hospitality, said goodbye and closed the door.

Then the comments began as one of the guys jokingly said to one of the ladies, "You know Angie, Bill said he wanted to keep you here and marry you if you're a willing."

The lady laughed and played along with the joke for the benefit of the others.

She indicated that he was rather attractive and that she would consider that.

On and on it continued as we began our taxi.

I cautiously back taxied up hill and noted my best departure ground-run route.

After all checks were completed, I lined up, began spooling up the engines and commenced my take off run.

All seemed normal as I continued to increase my power setting and as some know the Garret Engines have immediate thrust coming out the back.

Suddenly my right engine N1 gauge dropped significantly.

I immediately aborted, balancing some thrust reverse while avoiding the scattered rocks.

I managed to stop the aircraft and as the dust cleared went through a quick trouble shoot with no result.

Thinking it could possibly be a gauge problem and with seemingly balanced thrust and with zero maintenance around, I considered for a second to depart. However I decided to err on the safety side and taxied back. I found a good spot and went through my checks again.

I once again had an N1 drop at a high power setting and decided to get maintenance involved. We taxied back toward the ramp.

"What's going on Captain?" Someone called out.

"I've got a malfunction with a gauge I suspect, however, I don't want to chance that there could be another problem."

"I'll get Bill to make a call and get some maintenance out here within a couple of hours. If It's not repairable right away, they'll leave the mechanic and fly you on over to Anchorage."

"OK." Then there was silence as we approached the ramp area.

Then one of the passengers, trying to lighten the situation, "You know Angie, Captain Tony can marry you two."

"Get out of here!" she replied.

As we parked, shutdown and opened the door, Bill walked toward the plane. He saw the dust kicked up by the abort and was glad we made it ok.

After deplaning I carefully looked over the engine, found nothing and once again headed toward his office / home.

I asked about making a call to Anchorage for us to get maintenance headed our way. He said sure of course and we proceeded to his communications room.

He plugged in some jacks and proceeded to dial out to a relay operator.

After a few minutes and several attempts, he mentioned we were under a solar flare alert and it may be some time before we could get any communication but mentioned that we were all welcome to spend the night.

The ladies were now horrified and the guys continued their subtle jokes if by no other means by sideward glances.

After some discussion, Bill and I assured our passengers that he would continue to try dialing out every half hour.

Shortly everyone headed back outside.

Bill followed them out and pointed to some small aluminum buckets sitting on a shelf, "Why don't you all go up on that hillside right there and pick some blueberries for supper. I'll make us a pie."

"The bears typically don't come in this close," as he gestured toward the hill.

After some thought and looking at the alternative way to spend time, I was not surprised to see them each grab a bucket and head up the hill. The guys took off their jackets and draped them along with their ties on some outside weather beaten chairs. Now that was something else. There goes a group of government folks in business dress carrying buckets headed up the hill to pick blueberries in remote Alaska.

Meanwhile I spent some more time with Bill as he showed me around and talked about what kind of facility this used to be back in the 70's.

Well Blueberry picking lasted about an hour and they reappeared with buckets of blueberries! After about another hour had passed, Bill was finally able to get his call through and forwarded my message to the company.

About two hours later our Piper Navaho arrived with mechanics and parts.

They worked their magic, found the problem and sure enough I had all my gauges reading correctly and with normal power departed without incident.

I'm sure the folks are telling this story to all their grandkids even now.

What a remarkable time.

By the way. Farewell is a very interesting place. If you get a chance, read up on some of the happenings around this location. There's more detail about the town and its lone resident reflected in 'Once a Warrior – Captain Thomas Price – Mission Alaska.'

Regretfully it appears that all the buildings have been leveled and the materials dissipated or moved to another location. With the exception of the airstrip and occasional hunters flying in there doesn't seem to be any sign of life.

Sparravohn (SVW)

This LRRS U.S. Air Force Strip is located 188 miles from Anchorage. It has a 4,000-foot runway on the slope of a 3,200-foot mountain and an almost 5% runway gradient. You're surrounded by mountains with one way in and one way out. With a hill at the approach end and a small valley to negotiate on final it can be a challenge in the best of weather. Several accidents have occurred here with Flight Crews lost. The only runway gradient higher in Alaska is Indian Mountain LRRS at 7%. Both can be quite a challenge.

As weather allowed we landed here almost daily as part of our normal schedule.

Approach to landing was in general somewhat precarious to say the least. The addition of a moderate gusting crosswind and a rapidly lowering ceiling we knew could spell disaster.

It's a good idea to practice this approach to landing at low level on a good VFR day in case you need to have an escape route. That suggestion applies to many of the passes and other airstrips as well.

Once on the ground in winter be aware of the outside temperature as it can easily be 50 below even on a sunny day. Get your winter gear on before opening the cabin door which goes for anywhere out there in winter. We've had guys come back with frostbite simply because of a hole in their glove.

Lime Village (2AK)

Just 20 miles from Sparravohn, this village is located at a bend in the Stony River. The short runway is treacherous to say the least and seemed the worst during breakup. The River is ice free only about 4 months. Spent quite a lot of time there delivering supplies and groceries along with passengers in and out almost daily.

However, today I understand the Village is down to a population somewhere between six and twenty-five.

The only school in the village has closed more than once as the number of enrolled students dropped below the 10 student minimum required for funding by the state.

These remote villages are continuing to die out. Since the 90s, statistics show a decline of 86% primarily which I believe is due to the younger generation attending college in larger cities and not returning to village life after graduation.

43

Here's some maneuvering for you on this treacherous village strip. It was during break up and is an incident on an icy runway with 'good traction' for landing reported by the village Unicom.

'Glancing downward momentarily, I noticed the heavy ice flow in the river. As I established my base leg, I lowered flaps to full down position and began slowing to my minimum approach speed.

Now on final, I slowed to the very minimum speed and added a little power to keep from stalling while clipping the bushes at the end of the runway.

Just above stall speed now, I touched down the Seneca II exactly on the end of the 1,500-foot runway.

I held the nose off momentarily, looking for some aerodynamic braking, then gently lowered the nose and raised the manual flaps.

As I touched the brakes however.... we sped up!

I now began braking with rapid, on off brake pedal action. We were not slowing at all. 'This is not good!' I thought to myself!

I considered going around, but I wasn't sure of the condition of the remainder of the runway now. I could see standing water and possibly mud coming up and felt we might not get airborne. I certainly didn't want to go plowing through mud only to end up in the river.

I could see the other end of the runway now. What I was looking at was not a pretty sight. There was no barrier at the end of the runway. From there, the terrain sloped down a 30 foot embankment into the river flowing with ice.

I was still barreling toward the river and went back to full flaps... Got to try aerodynamics again... With full flaps, I lifted the nose off the runway. I wasn't slowing at all. Not good. Not good! The end of the runway and river was coming up fast.

I kicked the rudder full to the right, hoping to get traction in a side slide and maybe some aerodynamic drag from the tail. As I slipped to the side of the runway, I kicked full left rudder and began my slide to the right. I was slowing somewhat now but it still wasn't enough. I had one more action I could do besides going into the ice jammed river.

A ground loop seemed the best option. I knew it would damage the aircraft but anything was better than going down that river bank.

I kicked full right rudder and began to spin the nose around to the right. As I passed the 90-degree point, the river was all over my windshield!

I added some power to the left engine to continue my spin around. Our momentum toward the river seemed to be subsiding as we went around.

My natural reaction to this new tail slide and to stop the spin-around was to begin powering up the right engine. It was working. It stopped the spin-around action and our momentum toward the river. I felt I was somewhere near the edge of the icy river bank, not fully stopped, but now pointed in the right direction. I continued to push both throttles forward and was at full takeoff power.

That stopped my river-bound tail slide. Now stopped, pointed in the right direction, with engines roaring, we began moving back toward the ramp area!

Within three or four seconds, now moving rapidly toward the ramp, I had to chop both throttles in order to stop and prevent us from hitting the small embankment behind the turn out area.

We finally stopped in the turnaround area and were parked where we always parked. I pulled the mixtures back shutting down the engines. All was quiet.

Wow! I thought to myself. Using reverse thrust in a piston aircraft is not something one should try. But, if it keeps you and your folks out of the drink, especially one with icebergs all jammed together and everything, my feeling is do it! It worked that day!

As my passengers deplaned, not a word was said until the last passenger was getting out. She was about 75 I thought.

I steadied her by holding her arm as she stepped out on the ice-covered ground. She looked up, caught my eye and in broken English and with an unexcited voice," I didn't think we' za gonna make it."

"Yes Ma'am, it was a little bit slippery but... ahh, no problem!" I replied.

She held out her hand which I took gently and laid my other hand on hers with a warm gesture. She smiled, "Thanks. You can call me Mom now. Everybody else does."

I heard a heavy 'Thud!', 'Clunk!', 'Crack!' and the sound of rushing water. I knew it was the ice flow less than a hundred feet from where we stood.

As she turned and began walking away, I glanced over at the rumbling ice clogged river and let myself go there for a moment. I wondered... if you sink below the ice jammed river surface, how do you get back up through it? That is a tough one.' – (Excerpt from – Call Sign – 'Iceman)

Red Devil (RDV)

Located along the Kuskokwim River and about 250 miles west of Anchorage lies this very remote Athabascan and Yupik Eskimo village. I think there were only 25 or 30 folks living there during the 80's and 90's. The Red Devil Mine had closed some years before my time there.

Although it has a 4800 ft. airstrip, you might use caution in flying in there at any time. Like many of the villages along the Kusko this one is prone to flooding especially in spring due to ice jams damming the river.

These jams can form overnight so yesterday may not equal today.

Nikolai (FSP)

This Athabascan village is located 46 miles east from McGrath and about 250 miles west of Anchorage. Russian influence remains quite high here with the presence of a Russian Orthodox Church, their only church. There's lots of remains of Russian architecture of the period and although mostly Athabascan, many have names of Russian descent.

You might see a barge on occasion meandering up the river or dog sleds traveling on the dog sled trail in winter however most are dependent on air for food and supplies.

I became good friends with the Chief of the village after delivering mail and much needed supplies on a regular basis. He was the Postmaster as well as the leader of his clan. These are friendly folks but it's best to call ahead and let someone know to expect you.

Summer temperatures are moderate but in winter can drop well below zero in the neighborhood of - 50 / 60 degrees.

Although they work hard to keep the runway suitable, there are occasional snow berms that can be a challenge for any aircraft especially low wing aircraft.

Other than the runway in winter, possibly the greatest challenge is cold temperatures and whiteout conditions. The surrounding terrain, the lakes, the dog trail from McGrath, the Kusko River, and the village including every structure is

'WHITE'! Even light snow can be a real problem. There's a great 'White Out' Story at this village in – Call Sign 'Iceman'.

The very famous Iditarod Trail runs through the village and the runway can get quite busy during the Iditarod Race. Use caution here during any season.

McGrath (MCG)

McGrath was somewhat of a hub for us where we dispatched to various surrounding villages.

The entire area is quite susceptible to whiteout conditions in blowing snow and even with an ILS approach can be quite challenging.

One particular flight in our Beech 99 as we broke out at minimums our entire view was of a flat white landscape with only a VASI sticking its head out of the snow.

My First Officer stated "runway in sight" then followed with, "Is the VASI on the left or the right of the runway?"

It took a moment to think about that question, then we both stated "Left." Seconds later we picked up the faint lights of the runway and continued to an uneventful landing.

Best to be careful with Thrust Reversers with snow, you can easily put yourself in zero - zero conditions on the runway which could possibly ruin your day.

When flying IFR in the North Country, with temps commonly in the below zero numbers, don't forget to adjust your approach altitudes accordingly. (Check for the Snow Flake symbol and temperature restriction on the approach plate. Refer to NOTAM Cold Temperature Restricted Airports). Simply put, the colder it is the lower your true altitude may be.

Be very aware of temperature inversions in this area as well. It's easy to slip into an oil congealment incident. On one occasion my outside air temperature at 4,000 ft. was + 30 and on the ground was a – 40! That's a radical drop which does strange things to your aircraft windows and instrument faces not to mention your body when you step out of the aircraft.

Lose an engine in this area better be prepared to survive. One can succumb in just a few minutes without proper protection.

Red Dog Mine (DGG)

There's a lot of village strips marked (PVT) and they're generally serious about that.

However Red Dog was in a class by itself best described in those days as a hidden underground city with a gravel runway located in Inupiat territory.

When I was there the runway was a rough 3500 ft. strip located near the mine. There were trees at both ends and on the sides. It appears today their operation has radically expanded with trees removed and terrain changed. I can only imagine what their facility is like today.

My missions generally were to deliver personnel and supplies. However my most famous mission was to deliver Bruce Babbitt, then Secretary of the Interior for an inspection during the early days of the mining operation.

They were just getting started however their storage building over by the coast was touted as one of the largest buildings in the world at the time. That was about 25 years ago. Today this Lead and Zinc Mine has developed into a worldwide industry and employs many local people.

They now have a 6,000 ft. paved runway with Jet service!

Ruby (ARY)

Ruby's about 300 miles Northwest of Anchorage. This airstrip was decent, about 4,000 feet long and lies on top of a small mountain. It's about a mile from the main village set on the south shore of the Yukon River.

There's an RNAV approach today but prior we had to shoot the approach into Galena, cancel and proceed V.F.R. / I.F.R. (I Follow River) back to Ruby. Yes. A little more time but it usually worked out.

One of the interesting things I ran into at this village airstrip was that you have to pump your own fuel out of a barrel. You carry your own Chamois cloth and utilize a hand pump located on the barrel. Leave cash or a note as to number of gallons pumped.

Generally, no one was around however on one occasion, quite surprised, I observed another aircraft parked on the ground near the 'fuel farm'.

As I taxied up I immediately recognized him as my old Chief Pilot from Las Vegas! What a paradigm shift for us both – North Las Vegas Airport / Ruby Alaska?

"What in the world are you doing out here in the middle of the wilderness?"

Turns out he had a seasonal job with the U.S. Forest Service and was enroute to another village farther north. We really enjoyed kicking around some of the good old days but with tight schedules, shook hands and went our ways never to meet again.

On several occasions at this remote airport I loaded or unloaded alone and in a totally silent environment. Being in the middle of the wilderness sometimes instills a somewhat creepy feeling. In that regard I always laid my 12 Gauge just inside the door and didn't stray too far from it. Bears were always a consideration.

I was never charged by a bear there, however I was surprised twice at this airstrip by interesting humans.

On one particular day I'd just finished unloading my cargo and turned around to see a gray bearded old fellow approaching. My first thought was of St Nicholas complete with the white beard and alpine dress. He had a 5 ft. hiking stick and didn't seem very menacing at all.

We talked for some time and eventually I got around to asking him why he wasn't carrying a firearm in bear country.

"Sonny, I've had about 75 bear encounters here through the years. I just hit them across the snout with my stick and they run off."

Wow. I wasn't totally sure of his story but there he was and I knew there were plenty of bears around.

After talking a bit more, he said his goodbye and meandered off into the woods.

On another occasion, I'd landed at Ruby with several medium size barrels of diesel fuel.

I had just begun to adjust my ramp after maneuvering one of the heavy barrels to the edge of the doorway. Suddenly a large arm reached over my shoulder and grasped the edge of the barrel.

I spun around and discovered a tall dark Native American in native dress. He was dressed more Sioux than Athabascan and I took him to be one.

As a Vietnam Vet you bet I was surprised that he had come up behind me with absolutely no sound.

He said, "Let me help you get these off."

I said, "Sure. Thanks."

He was at least six foot two or three with long black hair almost to his waist.

51

Evidently quite strong, he proceeded to lift and sit out all four barrels.

Afterwards, he simply smiled, turned and walked back into the woods. Of course, I wanted to know more about both these men, however like many of the folks I've encountered, like a wisp of smoke, they vanished into the Alaskan Wilderness. I would never encounter them again but they remain well defined in my memory.

Holy Cross (HCR)

Holy Cross is a somewhat larger village located about 330 miles from Anchorage and adjacent to the mighty Yukon River. Primarily Native American, Yupik Eskimo and Ingalik Indian, this village seems somewhat progressive but has only +/- 200 total population.

Although Holy Cross folks are quite friendly use caution as you continue to venture up the Yukon River north. Be advised that the more remote you get, sometimes the less friendly the locals get.

There were other villages along the Yukon we serviced such as Grayling, Anvik, Shageluk and Russian Mission however I never felt connected for lack of a better term. I would use caution when operating in some of those areas.

I don't blame some of them actually for not liking outsiders as culture clash still exists in many parts.

For instance, although I agree there should be several areas of national parks in America, sometimes things aren't what they should be.

Wayne Westland, an Alaskan Native from northwest Alaska, described how his village was basically surrounded on three sides by national park in one day by the stroke of a pen in Washington D.C.

His people, Inuit, had lived, hunted and fished the ancestral lands adjacent to their village as far back as anyone could remember. To suddenly take away thousands of acres of land from their usage and subsistence to me is not exactly right. Yet, I guess the same thing occurred all across the U.S. as National Parks and other land designations took place. It just seems late in the millennia to still be doing that.

It's totally amazing that the plight of Native Americans in Alaska is still going on just like the Lower 48 in the past.

When you remove traditional hunting areas they have to adjust and become more dependent on subsidies and other government assistance.

Nome (NMN)

On over to the coast, about 500 miles from Anchorage and adjacent to the Norton Sound of the Bering Sea, lies the famous city of Nome. Of course, the Iditarod Mushers have to travel about 1,000 miles to get there and not at the speeds we have traveling by air.

One of my most interesting times there was again flying Bruce Babbitt, Secretary of the Interior in there as a stop on his tour of Alaska.

It was a very memorable occasion as we were met at the airport by about a 75 folks mostly dressed in native dress. They performed a native dance with exciting music and drums followed by a speech by one of the Elders.

That in itself was an awesome experience of a life time. I'm sure Bruce would agree.

However, in the evening I had a most memorable experience which occurred during the 'Potlatch' in the evening. As many know this is a dinner where everyone in the village contributes some local foods. Following a prayer of Thanksgiving we were invited to participate in the wide variety of food and drink.

After the main dinner we were invited to participate in the desert table. As guests we were all sitting together with the Secretary. I was next to him and we both pushed back our chairs and headed over for dessert.

The elders and other dignitaries followed us and as we picked out our desserts, they began conversing with him stopping us in our tracks. Meanwhile I reached in and loaded my small plate with some awesome looking Blueberry Cobbler.

Suddenly we became somewhat surrounded by these folks and I was standing next to the Secretary with my great looking dessert.

Attention seemed to focus on him allowing me to take a large bite of the Cobbler... A very big mistake.

I could not chew it, swallow it, or get rid of it. I felt like heaving... What a dilemma. Nowhere to go. Trapped next to the Secretary who was engaged in a political conversation. With mouth closed, I smiled with tight lips or nodded my head to answer any glances from anyone. Then, when no eyes were on me, I took one step back. Again, stood there in the crowd. Then when I had an opportunity, I took another step back.

Finally, I made it to a doorway, took one step back and saw a large trash can in the corner and as subtly as possible eased my plate into the trash and emphatically got rid of what I had thought was Blueberry Cobbler!

Survival Rule # 74 - Remember the blueberry cobbler you might run across in some of these villages is not the blueberry cobbler your mother made down in Georgia. A delicacy of the north, Eskimo ice cream, is made from seal oil, blubber, blue berries or other available berries and other unknown ingredients.

The hospitality of the Nome folks was unsurpassed. They struck me as warm, generous, friendly and very family oriented. I also remember the reverence before and during the prayer, as well as the humbleness, respect and graciousness Bruce demonstrated at the Pot Latch.

Hopefully no one's offended by the mentioning of different folks by their first names. It's just that the Alaska Frontier is a great equalizer of men. Many doctors don't want to be called Doctor. Pilots don't want any titles. Even some military officers wanted to be called by their first name, much like when you meet your maker I suppose. Something's very humbling about being deep in the Alaskan wilderness.

Wales (IWK)

Wales is an Inupiaq Eskimo village and the westernmost mainland city of Alaska and of the United States.

Just 18 miles from a Russian Island the village is very remote… Quite a run from Anchorage at about 600 miles.

Generally, most don't realize that the Arctic Circle just about identifies a country of its own. The top of the world has been inhabited by similar and related peoples for thousands of years. It only stands to reason when the ice is frozen, the dog trails become active and connect the land masses.

A lifetime resident and regular passenger, Nancy, an Inupiaq Native American lady and good friend, was born and raised in Wales. She always enjoyed riding right seat and conversing. One day we were discussing the "Wall coming down and the normalization of relations with Russia." She was born and raised only a few miles from the border. "Normalization?" she said in her Alaskan dialect. "Half my relatives live in Russia. We've been visiting each other as long as I can remember." Being in her 40's at the time, I believe that was long before the 'Wall came down.' In the winter, the narrow ocean between the Russian Island Big Diomede and the U.S. Island Little Diomede freezes solid allowing sled dogs and snow machines to travel back and forth. She also explained that every year Wales had a carnival with trading booths and were generally over-run by Russian relatives.

A most gracious lady, she presented me with a Hand-Woven Basket she had made. It's still on my shelf at home.

(These wonderful relationships I truly miss.)

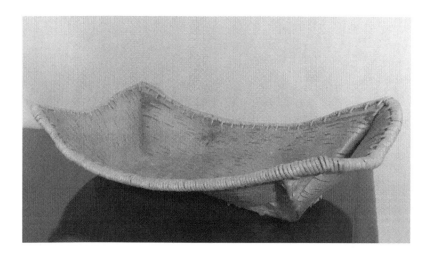

However, on the downside…

Wales can be interesting at times. I had quite an incident there presented in the upcoming Chapter 8 – 'Ambushed - Frontier Justice'.

All of us survived however the Pilot that helped us out of a fix did not. Next we continue east and over to the eastern border of Alaska.

Landing Along the Pipeline

On several occasions we had to fly to designated coordinates along the 'Haul Road' or Dalton Hwy to deliver supplies, parts or personnel. It's the only route to Prudhoe Bay and not a drive for the timid.

Our designated landing spot was usually a blocked off fairly straight portion of the road. The 'runway' was usually quite rough but adequate.

The guys were always glad to see us. Sometimes it meant one of them was headed back to Anchorage for a visit or to catch a flight back to the lower 48.

Temperatures can get quite radical in the winter. Winds can be as well especially when the Siberian Express is active, so one needs to take all precautions. Under any of those radical conditions everyone stays in the bunkers and we typically would not depart.

Not a lot of stories here with the exception of the fire in the outside toilet. Not on fire but they kept a flame going inside down below the seat. The one I remember seemed to be propane fed with a tube attached on top of a small metal plate hanging by a chain. Somewhat of a scary situation but it kept the outhouse tolerable at − 35 on a windy day. Wind chills there can exceed − 130 degrees. At − 45 you can take your fist and knock your fiberglass wingtip off.

A Treasure

Yes, there are sometimes adventures involved in Alaska flying. Yes, I have a Treasure Map. Can't say which village and who disclosed such an interesting story to me but here goes.

It goes back to the early 1900's and has to do with a trapper who for 20 years would only accept Gold Coins for his furs. The coins were never recovered. He lived alone in a cabin near the confluence of two streams and north of an abandoned village. I made notes of the general location and description of the cabin and the area surrounding it.

Sometime later, during a huge fire near Galena, I was regularly flying smoke jumpers and supplies north of the described area. After dropping them off I returned with an empty aircraft and decided to take a look along the same route and streams as described.

Utilizing various charts for topography, low and behold, on about the 4th day, I identified the ruins of the trapper cabin. It was totally overgrown and only visible from directly above. At least that part of his story was true.

The Trapper had told this young child now about 35 that he had buried the coins behind his cabin. That story and my subsequent discovery of the treasure area was 1986 or about 30 years ago.

I have not found anyone who would like to take on an expedition like this however it still seems feasible that no one has recovered the treasure. If my math is correct the trapper's story would have been around 60 years ago or about 1957. His Trapper friend was old at the time. So say Twenty-five years earlier would be in the 1930's. Gold coins of that vintage are worth many thousands each of course. However, the location is very remote with no facilities of any kind in the area. To fly over is one thing but to land one would need a helicopter. The river doesn't appear to be float plane friendly at all.

It's a logistics nightmare. Just to finance two helicopters with crews for clearing and metal detecting would be rather spendy as well thus the treasure if there will remain. Anyone for an adventure?

Northway (ORT)

Headed out to the northeast from Anchorage there's several airports and villages located along the way. The most memorable is Northway. Close to the Yukon Territory border it's a common Customs stop for many air travelers and the last stop before flying over to illustrious Dawson City.

The Northway area seems to have a considerably drier climate than most of Alaska and although in there many times I do not recall having to execute an instrument approach.

Runway surface conditions can vary with the seasons however wind on occasion was my greatest challenge. It is a nice and wide World War II airstrip built in the 40's.

Located near a glaciated river, the village is mostly Athabaskan and located just north of the airport. The people are hardy folks with long lifespans.

I had flown in there one day and heard that there was a lady that cooked the best apple pie in Alaska and had set up a small restaurant just down the road from the airport.

Wanting to stretch my legs somewhat, I ventured down that way and found her small Cafe with a screen door and Coke sign that reminded me of a small country store from my childhood down in Georgia.

I cautiously entered and noticed there were several very old Native Americans in one corner of the restaurant. I proceeded to the opposite corner table and sat facing outward – typical Vet.

The person behind the counter who turned out to be Nelly the owner, waved me over to the small counter and took my apple pie and coffee order. She carefully poured my coffee there. I thanked her and returned to my table.

A few minutes later, with heated apple pie in hand she came around the counter and brought the desert to my small table.

I thanked her and began eating my delicious slice of pie while glancing occasionally at these old - old folks just finishing up their meal. They conversed quietly in Athabaskan occasionally looking at me.

After signing their ticket, the 4 ladies and 1 man methodically began standing and helping each other to depart their table.

As they headed to the door, I could see they might need some help so I laid my napkin on the table and proceeded to open the door for them.

As the seemingly 80 – 90 year old's passed by they smiled and thanked me.

When the last one, an old bent over leathery faced man, passed by, he stopped and turned to look at me then put out his large strong hand.

I took his hand. He looked into my eyes and gave me a strong handshake, "Thank you very much!"

"You're certainly welcome sir."

He then turned and joined the waiting ladies.

I returned to my table and continued with my apple pie and coffee.

Nelly came over with some fresh coffee, "That was very nice of you to hold the door open for them. Do you know who that was?"

"I sure don't."

"That was Chief Northway, his Daughter and two Grand Daughters. The youngest is 95. The Chief is either 130 or 140 depending on who you ask. There were no tribal records kept in those days. He's the one who established our Village a long time ago."

ALASKA PILOT'S THANKSGIVING

What an awesome privilege it was for me to fly through your beautiful mountain passes, over the vastness of your tundra and to see your pristine rivers, lakes and islands.
I've soaked into my soul the canvas of the soft pastel colors of your skies touting the complete spectrum of the colors of the rainbow.
I've sailed along past your majestic snowcapped mountains and seen a thousand of your beautiful sunrises and sunset of yellows, gold and reds sometimes at the stroke of midnight.
I've sailed along your aqua blue, sometimes emerald green waters shown with the brilliant whiteness of the ice, your crystal-clear rivers, tranquil in places, were often raging as they weaved through your pristine wilderness.
I've seen first-hand the unstoppable forces of nature humbling even the bravest and heartiest of souls.
I've watched as millions of birds all arose at the same time, changing the colors of the landscape from green and blue to white.
I've shared days with kindred Alaskan people, sadness and loss, but also happiness and good cheer.
Thank you Alaska for sharing your Great Land, your Wonderful People, your mystery and your challenge.

Thank you God for allowing me to be there and to become an integral part of your beautiful creation. Amen.

Tony Joyner
Jan. 28, 199_

Chief Northway, Founder of the Northway Village was widely Revered throughout Alaska. Meeting this gracious and wonderful man is one of the most memorable highlights of my career as a pilot in Alaska. This plaque was created to pay Honor and Tribute to this Great Leader of his people.

Wow. You never know who you might run into in the great Alaska Wilderness, even stopping for pie and coffee.

What a privilege it was to have met and to have spoken with this very Revered Athabaskan Chief,

Chief Walter Northway
1876 – 1993

An 'Elder of Elders' – Cheryl Silas

(Northway Village Council)

Chapter Five

FLYING THE SOUND

There are tons of stories that occurred in the Sound as we were in there somewhere almost every day. My best description of the Sound is that on some days you feel like you should have bought a ticket.

It is one of the most scenic wilderness areas in Alaska with the Blue waters, White Snowcapped mountains, Beautiful Glaciers spilling into the sea, and Birds by the millions flocking around the beautiful islands. Just a few of the magnificent sights ...

Then,

There are some days that are so dangerous with icy winds and weather that you're just not getting paid enough for being there!

Single Engine

I wouldn't recommend flying across the Prince William Sound single engine without floats although I've done it many times.

If you elect to travel across to Cordova or Valdez plan to cross just as you would fly over a mountain range.

Why? There's nowhere to land in that Sound should you develop engine trouble. I take that back. There are about 3 strips available... Hinchinbrook Island if you're headed to Cordova.

Johnstone Point built for the VOR maintenance crews. Landed a C206 there. It's Short, sandy and soft but an okay runway for large tires. Another is Tatitlek where we flew into almost daily.

Okay. Single Engine - Still going...? Take a look at your performance charts and especially your glide ratio. Adjust for the age and condition of your aircraft. For instance, you might need to cross at 12,000 feet or higher mid-channel to make it to any decent landing spot especially toward Valdez. Much lower and you're betting your life that your engine will not have a problem. There's not much available, just rocks that dive straight into the ice-cold water.

OK, you say yours is a new aircraft or engine and chances of losing an engine are pretty remote. Want to bet your life and others lives on it?

If you do have an engine problem and have to land or crash land on or near any of these islands, be aware. There's plenty of Bears.

On one occasion flying along the islands low level in our Piper Seneca II from Cordova I observed two Brown Bears swimming from one island to another. Yes, they can swim! It's their islands. Are you prepared to survive a Bear attack?

Here's a dilemma to consider. Put it on a rocky shore – damage – injured probably. Prepare to defend yourself after a few hours. Put it just off the beach in the water – Prepare to swim in ice water for 8 to 10 minutes. T.U.C. say 4 or 5 minutes? You're almost to shore and there are two Brownies turning over rocks looking for something to eat. But, not to worry, they won't eat you just kill you. They don't like the taste of us in any way.

The following are some experiences and highlights of some of the hazardous conditions you possibly will encounter in this beautiful but deadly part of Alaska.

Cordova (CDV)

This is a beautiful, small and friendly city set by Orca Bay in the Sound, home of the Ice Worm Festival and a great place to visit. I spent many hours and occasional nights there with some really great friends.

On the downside the weather can change radically with lots of snowy weather. It seemed to be a rare occasion when we could get in VFR.

There were many harrowing flights into and out of there especially in the darkness of winter. Here's an example of a hazardous situation that occurred one ice and snow filled night.

As we approached Cordova it seemed late at night – however probably 7 PM - in our B99. Yes, it can be very dark at 7 PM especially when the old Low is in the center of the Sound. We were flying in moderate occasionally heavy snow and high winds.

The preferred runway with winds out of the southwest was serviced only by an NDB approach which was well below minimums. We had to elect the ILS with a Circling approach which seemed suitable.

We received vectors to final meanwhile taking on ice and encountering more moderate snow.

As we intercepted the Final Approach Course, we immediately blew by the Final Approach Fix, executed the missed approach and asked for another approach.

Realizing we had 50 or 60 knots on the tail on final we planned for a somewhat steeper approach. We intercepted the final further out and slowed immediately.

The snow showers had somewhat let up and we picked up the approach lights at the Final Approach Fix. However, with the turbulence and up and down drafts it soon appeared and felt that we were stationary and the approach lights were moving up and down, left and right.

Both were experiencing vertigo and knew it would take good crew coordination to get to the runway safely.

As we both realized the phenomenon, I committed solely back to concentrating on instruments with my copilot looking at the runway.

We managed to get down to our circling altitude and began our offset turn back around to final.

Once there we had about 25 knots on the nose and our landing on the icy snow-covered runway was smooth and uneventful.

It's a good practice to check where the Low-Pressure centers are located adjacent to your route especially in the Sound. Plan accordingly. A low pressure centered in the sound will give you tremendous tailwinds on the ILS in Cordova along with the very rugged weather that goes along with it.

In that regard, I've had close to 90 knots on the tail when transitioning to the Valdez LDA/DME approach from Johnstone Point.

Vertigo – I've encountered this phenomenon several times through the years but obviously have corrected with Instrument Flight. I'm still here.

Especially at low level this potential hazard whether IFR or VFR is quite dangerous and can be fatal. When there is fog or snow falling on glassy water or at night when the horizon is absent the possibility for Vertigo is quite strong.

Takeoff and initial climb is one of the most dangerous. Why… Because of engine torque, P factor, and entering possible turbulent conditions or wind shift just above the surface.

If caught up in that situation and you've lost the horizon, instantly revert to instruments. Lock on! They were working before and are not lying to you! Vertigo can happen to anyone. If not handled quickly, this phenomenon can be a killer.

Alaska can be a black hole at night. No pilot is immune from spatial disorientation. Watch your altitudes even adjacent to the airport. Case In Point - a C 130 landed on the downwind leg at Prudhoe Bay. Flat light – Snow. Somebody needs to be on the gauges in those conditions.

Valdez (VDZ-PAVD)

It's a beautiful setting for this Coastal City adjacent to the pyramid shaped snowcapped mountains.

However, …

SNOW / ICE / WIND / ROCKS is another way to describe Valdez. Most accidents are fatal here.

There again, you have ice cold water with floating ice burgs, 4,000-foot rocks everywhere and rapidly changing weather.

However, some of the fond memories are of flying enroute low level across the face of the Columbia Glacier and observing the seals playing on the icebergs. They're good surfers as I've seen them catch a wave on a small berg and move right along. Of course, pods of Orcas cruise around just below the surface.

However, if you do elect to fly into Valdez at low level there's a couple of items you should know.

You need to know the coastline extremely well to identify the correct canyon-like Fiord to go into. It's easy to be a little off course especially with the strong Sound winds and possibly proceed up the wrong one. Of course, they're dead-ends, so regardless always leave room to turn around.

(What's a Fiord you ask? Well, for us airmen, they're a series of dead-end water filled canyons that open into the larger body

67

of water. The large canyons were carved by giant glaciers that once covered the region.)

During the late 80's and early 90's we had company specific FAA Approval for a VOR DME Visual approach into Valdez which generally worked out well. It was utilized for example when the 4000-foot minimums prevented us from landing when the ceiling was actually just below that.

On occasion following an icy and harrowing missed approach on the LDA we had to travel back to the VOR at Johnstone Point and request our Company VOR approach.

'One such missed approach occurred when an un-forecast snow storm occurred. I began taking on a ton of ice just before the missed approach point. I had a full load of anxious passengers. I could not believe this was happening as the forecast was for 5,000 foot ceilings and 10 miles visibility. At 50 feet above minimums, I began powering back up. At MDA (minimum decision height) I was at full power, covered with ice, climbing at best only 500 feet per minute, in turbulence and heavy snow.

Using extreme caution, I slowly began my turn around. You betcha' I was sweating bullets - again. The engines were roaring, ice was piling up on the windshield. Glancing quickly to the side, I cycled the boots. All de-ice was working properly it seemed. I slowly began climbing out. The hazard is that anytime you get your aircraft contaminated with ice, especially the wings, your performance drops and your stall speed increases dramatically.

As the pelting ice and snow slowly diminished and things got more under control, I called back to the station. The ceiling was 1,800, visibility now 7 miles. That was good news to me. Those conditions made the VOR Approach from over the Johnston Point suitable.

That was another company specific instrument approach we were authorized to fly. That approach simply let you down over the water at a certain altitude outside the Narrows with room to turn around in case you couldn't proceed VFR. This was a valuable tool when the ceilings were below the high LDA minimums. However, this approach had one or two drawbacks. You could get three miles visibility and cancel which to me was a pretty risky option. Three miles over the water is not that great for finding your way along the coastline.

About 20 minutes later, after negotiating the VOR approach, I was arriving at the Narrows at 1,500 feet. I was able to hold that altitude as I hugged the rock wall on the right. Again, I began encountering snow, visibility began to drop. Down to four or five miles now, I was straining for my visual checkpoints. I additionally had my NAV set to the LDA final which I began receiving. Centered up on that, I finally identified the snow-covered runway and announced my intention to land. Glancing back toward the narrows I could only see whiteness. It felt good to be home. As I lined up on the runway and began easing the throttles back, I could hear several general sighs of relief from the back. As I touched down in the smooth snow-covered runway a nice general round of applause broke the silence. It seemed like some of them had been through that before. As I taxied in toward the terminal, the ramp agents came jogging out toward the airplane. I had already shut down the left engine as I rolled to a stop. Stopped now, I completed my shutdown checks quickly. The ramp agent opened the door and began assisting people off the plane. Now it's my turn to let down. As I walked toward the terminal behind the last of the folks, I glanced upward, whoops, forgot for a second. Realization began to set in. I've got to either find my way through the narrow rock walled canyon or climb up through this mess if I'm going to get back to

Anchorage tonight. After a short delay and a couple of coffees, the ceiling lifted just enough to meet departure minimums. I quickly got the passengers aboard and after a good briefing including the "possibility of some weather" enroute, I started the engines and began taxiing to runway 24. Pre-takeoff checks complete, I pulled out the departure plate for a quick review.

'Piece of Cake', I thought.

"Everyone ready?" I asked. I was pleasantly surprised at the visibility at this point. The snow had ended. Takeoff and climb were normal and we headed to Anchorage.' (Excerpt - Call Sign – Iceman)

Mark, one of our outstanding Pilots came up to me on the ramp at Merrill Field one afternoon.

"It works, it really works!"

You can only peer so far inside the narrows and once you go around the bend you're committed, you have nowhere to go. There's just not enough room to make a safe 180 once committed.

He had actually ran into this dreaded trap around the bend in the narrows. The airport weather was reported VFR with a fifteen-hundred-foot ceiling at the airport. The Narrows were reported clear. However, there it was… a low fog bank ahead.

"Just like we practiced the other day, I intercepted the Localizer and tracked it to the runway!"

Training for the worst scenarios on VFR days is a good practice.

Just a small note about IFR into Valdez… There's been several fatal accidents in IFR conditions including Air Force aircraft. So stay on your game, don't take any chances and have a backup plan.

Another is to be aware of your height above terrain along the approach path, not referring to the HAT (Height above

Touchdown). If you look at the Valdez approach plate you can see that at Paydi Intersection you're in the vicinity of 6,000 ft. terrain! Crossing altitude 6,400 feet.

It's easy to feel you've got a lot of room under you with a 6,000 ft. number on the plate. You don't have 6,000 feet to play with!

Never break those altitudes given. Regretfully some haven't taken those numbers seriously with disastrous results.

Add a terrain hazard to a 75-knot crosswind on the localizer at that altitude and you get a very deadly mix.

One additional note and that is during fishing season be aware of and watch for low level aircraft buzzing in patterns above fishing vessels. Fish spotters are usually good pilots but are operating 1500 feet or lower with a specific agenda of locating large schools of Salmon.

Chapter Six

KENAI PENINSULA
Southern Cook Inlet

Kenai, Soldotna and Homer are typical destinations south of Anchorage however there's many airstrips scattered along the way. Fantastic panoramic views are in every direction flying along the mountains. Some of the passes in the mountains are simply pristine.

Multiple airstrips and land-able beaches are found all along the Cook Inlet shoreline as well. I've landed on several. Great Clamming and fishing however, just as mentioned earlier use extreme caution landing on shorelines of Turnagain Arm or the Knik Arm for that matter... Not a good place to become stranded.

While you're flying down the Kenai Peninsula don't miss a landing at Homer and possibly take a boat over to Halibut Cove.

A great day trip is down to Homer, have lunch or dinner then return to Anchorage via the Harding Ice Fields.

Homer itself has a unique "spit" that extends 4.5 miles into the Kachemak Bay with several nice restaurants and quaint shops. The Lands' End hotel has a view that's incomparable.

I've landed at one or two of the airfields across the bay with a Cessna 206 and wouldn't recommend anything else.

All the airstrips are very short and require good power to get out of the mountainous area. It's generally best to take a float plane over if possible.

The dangers are typical Alaska with rapidly changing weather as the main culprit.

Ice as in the first Commuter crash is one of the major hazards however winds can play a part even on blue sky days.

For instance, I had a Private student on her long cross-country solo flight inbound to Anchorage from Homer in a Cessna 152. Through her ongoing calculations discovered she had severe headwinds in excess of 55 knots. All the forecast winds were 15 to 20 knots at her planned altitude. Although she would be somewhat late upon her planned arrival, I was relieved that she had the wisdom to land in Soldotna, make a phone call and take on fuel as a precaution, a wise move indeed.

If you're headed north, low on fuel and looking out the windshield at the Turnagain Arm… Land somewhere. Take on fuel. Live to fly another day.

Therein lies another accident along the same route concerning a pilot returning to Anchorage with his family in a Cessna 206. He'd fought headwinds all the way up and perhaps they were late for some planned engagement.

Remember in a descent with turbulent conditions that remaining fuel could slosh away from your fuel intakes. That 1/8 of a tank showing suddenly went to 0.

No matter the exact cause, the engine quit as he began his descent into Anchorage. They landed slightly offshore. Unable to swim to safety in the ice-cold water, the occupants all drown.

If you're low on fuel or even have a question, land, spend the time, and take on the extra fuel. So it'll cost you a $1.00 more a gallon, isn't your life worth more than 15 dollars?

It's not just in Alaska. That type incident happens everywhere. Why do people gamble like that? I have no idea.

Another peeve I have with pilots, even experienced pilots, is the tendency to attempt to stretch a glide when you're over water or over a remote area.

If flying commercially it's better to be looking for another job than attempt to save a company aircraft. Crash-land the sucker, go ahead, tear the landing gear off, sever the wings between two trees. ***Keep forward speed*** even if it means splashing down in icy water.

There were two Navajo accidents in the area where good pilots did not survive. Both of the following fatals were obviously caused by the aircraft flying too slow in an emergency situation.

The first was caused by the pilot trying to stretch a 'glide' single engine that is with one engine caged. Believe me, most twins when heavily loaded are only capable of slowing your descent. Without maintaining a decent airspeed, the good engine will simply lead you to the crash site.

It was piloted by a friend I'd flown with and have written about a few times. Jim had survived a C119 sabotage accident described in Chapter 8 "Ambushed – Frontier Justice". He was not so lucky in this crash.

He was a good pilot and you wonder why he didn't survive this one.

He'd just departed the Kenai airport with 7 passengers aboard, lost an engine shortly after takeoff and didn't have much time with a reported 300– 400 feet altitude. My guess is that with 7 passengers and fuel he was close to gross weight. He announced his engine out and he was returning for a landing. The suspected VMC rollover occurred just short of the airport. There were six fatals including the pilot. Two miraculously survived. One of the surviving passengers related that the stall warning buzzer was going on and off just before the crash. The plane went inverted into a house close to the runway. An explosion and fire occurred shortly thereafter. VMC Rollover? I believe so.

The other Navajo had just departed Kodiak and had a nose baggage door pop open. He announced returning to the runway and in his turn stalled and crashed. He had 9 fishermen aboard and I assume all their gear. That's heavy with any amount of fuel aboard. There were 6 fatals including the pilot.

The aircraft was recovered and appeared that it had entered the water almost vertically.

Granted being over that ice cold water would really make you want to stretch your glide to Terra Firma. A controlled water landing could possibly have been survivable whereas trying to fly a gross weight Chieftain close to stall speed with a baggage door open is guaranteed not to be.

These were tragic and no one really knows what pilot actions, his observations or thinking processes were but the evidence indicates flying at a critical airspeed in both emergency situations.

Splash down! Don't die stretching! Fly the numbers – Only… Take your chances in the water. The other route is guaranteed terminal.

I always tell my guys – Airspeed control is what will keep you alive. I've experienced several engine losses, one at rotation on a short runway as well as had a couple of baggage door openings. Airspeed control is the only thing that saved my rear end. I mean +/- 5 knots can make a difference.

These two accidents could possibly have been survivable.

One reads about baggage doors and fatalities all the time.

It is highly distracting but you must focus your attention on #1 – Airspeed control. That incredible induced drag can bleed off airspeed in seconds. Also, if you're encountering buffeting even at a hundred knots, accelerate to 110 or 120 to enable a controlled decent.

A VMC rollover can also happen quickly folks. You do not want to encounter either at low level. My take is that if the aircraft is still descending 300 feet per minute at Vxse, you're at best in a glide for an off-airport landing. Stay away from redline! Don't go below Vxse (Best Angle of Climb Single Engine) for any reason. If you're capable fly Vyse - Blue Line (Best Rate of Climb SE) to hold altitude. If a climb is encountered get higher or accelerate as you can especially in turbulent conditions. Airspeed is your only friend here.

I personally know of several fatal accidents due to baggage doors coming open. Cause of crash... Failure to maintain airspeed in both single and multi-engine aircraft accidents.

An open cabin or baggage door should never cause a fatal crash.

These accidents are usually due to failure of the pilot to maintain air speed leading to a stall accident. If it pops, forget about it and fly your airplane. Maintain airspeed even if you're flying 'a Brick' to the surface. Keep forward momentum. Fly until your wheels are on the ground or on the water. You might walk away.

Here is another detail that might just save your neck someday.

So, you're flying a brick at the best angle or rate of climb in a 250 FPM rate of descent.

You're over water or flat terrain.

Ever heard of Ground Effect? As you slide into it you might just level out enough to limp to a decent landing area or beach. Still not working, go ahead and contact at a reasonable speed above stall.

It's rather simple.

Baggage door pops open, Maintain Forward Momentum.
You might just walk or swim away.
Stall the aircraft. You Die!

<u>Always</u> Keep Forward Momentum.
Fly until your wheels are on the ground or in the water.

Chapter Seven

FLYING THE ALEUTIAN CHAIN

There are a lot of obvious hazards involved in flying down the chain.

Having flown many charter flights and medivacs in and out of Cold Bay, Dutch Harbor and as far west as Attu my most vivid memories are of cold, cold winds, Ice, tight approaches, points of no return, water, water everywhere and almost forgot – active volcanoes.

When the volcanoes are active you have to plan accordingly depending on winds aloft and the direction of the plumes. There were usually one or two active volcanoes somewhere along our routes.

Case:

My friend Wayne Brockman, who I had flown with and occasionally followed through all types of weather and situations, had moved on to another carrier flying out of Cold Bay.

No one knows how Wayne ended up on the rocks near Leonard Harbor in the Cold Bay vicinity. He was enroute from Cold Bay to King Cove. The weather was overcast but VFR below. The speculation is that the ceiling came down to the water during his flight.

79

Of course, he would have climbed up to get reception from the few navigational aids in the area. He would have also climbed above any obstacles, such as the protruding, two-thousand-foot Rock Mountains charging out of the sea. He would have climbed in a direction so as to avoid terrain at all costs, which I'm sure he was.

However, one of the phenomena I've found, flying along the Aleutian Chain, is that one can experience a ninety to one hundred eighty-degree wind shift which sometimes occurs right at the base of a cloud layer.

For example, I was on an NDB approach into Dutch Harbor (no GPS in those days) with marginal weather and high winds as usual. I had an extreme right crosswind on the final approach course estimated to be sixty or seventy knots. As I broke out of the clouds, looking out the windshield, all I could see was a rock wall. I quickly looked to my left, and realized I had flown a wind correction crab angle of more than sixty degrees. Now, the wind had shifted one hundred eighty degrees, and I was now being blown toward the rock wall. I swung the nose around immediately to compensate.

I later discussed the phenomenon with several other pilots where I heard of a fatal accident that had occurred on this same approach. A light twin aircraft, with four FAA Inspectors aboard, had flown straight into that rock wall. My guess is that the radical wind shift along with poor visibility was the primary cause. If I had not broken out when I did or had continued with poor visibility, I could easily have become another statistic. The cloud ceiling and layer, along with the moderate turbulence, was being caused by two rapidly moving air masses colliding at about two thousand feet.

Had I not broken out would I have realized a wind-shift had occurred in time to correct? I don't know. The rocks are gray and blend in perfectly with the clouds and fog.

It was an extreme situation and adds respect to the minimums designed into the approach charts. Respect them! My feeling was that I had less than two minutes to make a decision before slamming the rocks.

Wayne I'm sure was a victim of this or a similar extreme weather phenomenon. He was in the vicinity of those vertical rock islands. The ceiling possibly fell down onto the water, leaving him no alternative except to climb out. He began climbing in the direction he knew would let him avoid the rocks. However, with a one hundred eighty-degree wind shift, at a velocity of sixty or seventy knots or greater, in IMC (instrument conditions), he could have easily drifted away from his window of opportunity to escape.

His Piper Navajo aircraft was spotted the next day within a few feet of the top of the tallest rock spire.

A Somewhat Morbid Story
On A Dark and Rainy Night for the 'Chain Gang'

Normally our Medevac Missions were to save lives.

However, this night we were dispatched in our Conquest II to a remote island airport down the Aleutian Chain to pick up three deceased men. There were no nurses or technicians sent along with us.

After a harrowing icy middle of the night flight down the 'Chain', we executed an NDB approach, turned on the runway lights remotely, then surprisingly we actually found the runway.

We arrived around 3:00 AM and as we taxied into the ramp area saw three large green body bags in our taxi lights. We shut down nearby. There were no lights on the ramp and no one around at all. The men evidently were not locals.

There was no terminal building, just a small shack which was padlocked. With flashlights we examined the three body bags and located our paperwork in a plastic pouch attached.

It was raining heavily now and pitch dark. We were freezing cold but got to the task.

We were totally freaked out as in some horror movie but continued to struggle for 30 minutes working those bags up and into the cabin. All were large men with the largest at about 240 lbs.

We had all aboard finally and for weight and balance concerns had placed two on one stretcher on the right side.

I slipped forward stripping my wet jacket and began the checklist to get our aircraft started. Charlie had closed the door and was continuing to secure our 'passengers'.

Just as I was about to start, I felt a thud in the back. Then heard screaming and yelling like I'd never heard. I quickly aborted the start.

Charlie had slipped on the wet muddy floor and accidently pulled a 210 lb. body bag right on top of him.

He couldn't get up from the narrow, wet Aisle and was pinned to the floor.

I unbelted and grabbed the top of the body bag while the screaming continued.

With both of us struggling he finally managed to wiggle out the back toward the door.

"Charlie, You alright?" I questioned.

I shined the flashlight onto his white face as he sat on the wet floor.

"I'm sick. I got to get out," as he reached up and released the door.

He stood then slid down the air stair door and disappeared into the rainy night.

I carefully stepped toward the back and down the stair as well and found him bent over and heaving.

As I approached him he waved his arms and stood in the rain now looking up.

I didn't know if I had a patient to rescue or what.

"Charlie, You Okay?"

Suddenly and quietly, he let out a soft chuckle. Then I knew he was ok.

Then we both had a go at laughing it off while standing in the rain. It seems we both needed an outlet to relieve the stress. After a couple of minutes we were getting rain soaked.

"I'm ok, we better get out of here," he said quietly.

"Yea," I replied.

We both got our wits back, eased back into the aircraft, closed the door.

I went forward, stepped carefully around the large bag on the cabin floor, then we both lifted it carefully into place.

I assisted in the securing until we were positive there would be no further surprises.

It felt good to be belted in the cockpit and taxiing out.

We once again shifted our attention to the black night, the short gravel runway, the cold white capped waters not so far in front of us.

We had a normal takeoff, encountered moderate icing as usual, got through that and soon were on top with an unbelievable starlit night.

"Don't worry Charles. I won't ever tell that story."

"Thanks."

I guess I lied.

We were totally respectful before and totally respectful after the incident and were very glad to put that mission behind us.

God speed those who are carrying on today.

Chapter Eight

AMBUSHED - FRONTIER JUSTICE

As a tourist in Alaska, you get to see and experience a lot of course. You are, however, in a somewhat protective and controlled environment. There is an Alaska, as you know by now, that would take one years to see, to know, and to understand. The following story, incident, and accident further expose some not so good sides of some who have lived there.

As I've mentioned previously, make sure you're invited to any of the remote Native Villages before you drop in. Most are very friendly, but it is still customary to make a phone call or two if you have some business there. Many villages are very private and may not appreciate your presence.

It was the peak of summer, when I was sent to pick up a passenger from the small village Crooked Creek located on the Kuskokwim River. This one turned out to be a female school teacher who had been trying to leave for days. The weather had not been cooperating, and had left the short, rough runway very muddy. I used every precaution as usual and safely got in and out with no problems.

The young and attractive lady was quite talkative on the way to Anchorage and was very glad to be headed to civilization. Among other things discussed, we spent some time just talking about life in a Native American village. She had lived there over two years. It was all very interesting and I was amazed at some of the things that went on in everyday life there. Other than isolation, one of the things she had been uncomfortable about was the fact that the people primarily lived by tribal law. She related a few stories about some various incidents that resulted in some harsh judgment and punishment.

One particular story was that the tribal council had judged one of their own as guilty of killing another man in the village. His sentence, or punishment, was to be "walked" down to the river and to be banished from the tribe forever.

At first glance, it didn't sound like much of a punishment. However, when I factored in the remote location of the village, the sub-zero temperatures, with no weapons or anything to hunt with, and with only a light jacket, it became clearer. I'm sure this is just one example and the tip of the iceberg as far as justice carried out on the frontier.

Guy's, this is vast country. If you choose to explore the wilderness, I suggest you remember that 911 may not and most likely will not work. Satellite phone you say? That would be great, however, in a life or death emergency, the only one that can save your hide is yourself. The Alaskan Troopers are about as good as they come. It's just that it takes time to travel a hundred miles or more. My point is that you may be face to face dealing with some form of frontier justice. It's best to remember that in your planning and in packing your survival gear.

A good friend of mine, Jim Devine from a previous chapter, had a crash in a C-119 at a remote village near a mining operation. They were flying in much needed supplies for the miners, utilizing the village strip. The aircraft was heavily loaded with construction materials, groceries, and fuel. Conditions were good however, the ground was snow covered.

As they touched down, they saw a ripple on the snow-covered runway coming up fast. Before they could react, the landing gear was violently, and completely ripped from the fuselage. Now, they were two guys in a ninety-knot sled, full of cargo, headed for the trees. They went into the trees, shed the wings, down a slope, bounced off some rocks, and ended up in a ravine.

They quickly unbelted and climbed out of the smoking aircraft. Jim tested his legs and was surprised he could walk. They looked each other over. Neither was badly hurt, just stunned as to what just happened and what could have happened. They began limping back up toward the runway.

In Jim's sense of humor, "Well, Bill, that must have been a good landing. I've always been told that any landing you can walk away from is a good landing." Bill wasn't impressed with Jim's humor about the situation.

Some of the miners arrived shortly and helped clean up the mess. What they found was that someone had taken a piece of equipment, moved some rock and dirt just beyond the touchdown zone of the runway, packed it to the consistency of concrete, then concealed it by shoveling snow over it. The guilty parties were never found. The shell of the aircraft is still somewhere in the trees.

Two years later I had an incident at another village, this time on the northwest coast - Wales, Alaska... I'm not sure of the cause, or the situation, as we never found out who did it or why.

I had some government folks aboard from Anchorage that had to get to this village. I didn't know what organization or what their business was, only that they needed to get there in a hurry.

After a normal flight, I approached overhead the runway as usual, looking for traffic, checking the windsock for wind direction, and also the condition of the runway surface. At first glance the dirt runway looked clear. However, there seemed to be an unusual line dividing the runway in half.

Always checking for any irregularities I decided to slow down and make a low pass over the runway.

I alerted the passengers of my intention and lowered the flaps to approach. I extended the landing gear as I approached the end of the runway. Remaining just off to the right, I looked at the runway with scrutiny. I couldn't believe my eyes.

There was a three-foot berm, effectively dividing the short runway in half. This deadly berm I believe was designed to cause a crash for me and my passengers as the barrier was covered with the same-colored dirt as the runway.

There were no customary X's or any other obstacle on either end of the runway that would indicate that the runway was closed. There was no communication available with the village. Now, we're in the middle of nowhere, cannot land at our destination and possibly facing some hostility.

I retracted the gear and flaps, informed the passengers of our situation, and climbed to a safe altitude to hold our position. During the discussion of the situation, my passengers asked if there were any other airports in the vicinity. After searching the charts for a minute, I found an abandoned forestry strip that might be suitable.

This strip was located twenty-five miles away, but I thought I would take a look. After a few minutes of searching, we found the strip, which had a couple of structures, a fire tower, and possibly a phone. I carefully made two low passes over the strip looking for rocks, holes, or any type obstacle that might cause a problem for our landing or takeoff. We landed without incident, and began our search for a phone. I remember the very tenuous climb up a rotten fire tower ladder with one of my passengers. We found an old phone but it didn't work.

It'd been about an hour and with options running out, I heard the drone of an airplane. I quickly headed to the radio, and made a contact with Jim Smith. He was very friendly, cordial, and willing to help out my guys.

We stood and watched him circle over the field, then land in his Cessna 206 which obviously could land a little shorter than my Conquest II.

He was tall, sandy haired, athletic and looked more like a college football player than a bush pilot. He had been working for another carrier in the area, had some time, and would be happy to shuttle my guys over to the village. By making two trips, he felt he would be light enough, and could easily land his aircraft on half of the strip. On his return, he said there was no one at the airport and he didn't know who or why someone had blocked the runway.

"You definitely would have crashed," he commented.

I offered to pay him for his trouble but he refused. He was just glad to be able to help someone out. I planned to reward him somehow and took his name and contact number.

I waited until he was airborne on the second shuttle flight before thinking about getting out of there myself.

Standing there on the isolated forestry strip I watched as he went out of sight. I continued to listen to his engine echoing through the hills, then fade out to silence.

As the silence sank in I realized I was alone, totally alone. That is a strong, somewhat overwhelming and eerie feeling by the way. Some of you may know that feeling after being dropped off in the wilderness by a bush plane.

Convinced that my people were in good hands and about 5 minutes later, I climbed aboard my Conquest, closed the door and shortly was roaring down the runway headed to Nome for fuel.

A few days later, I attempted to get in touch with Jim. However, regretfully he had been killed in an aircraft accident somewhere near the village. No one seemed to know much about it but one fellow I spoke with said he heard there was a control cable break.

Upon investigation, I heard that no one knew who was responsible for my incident either, only that it "had happened before".

That simply reinforced a rule I generally use. <u>Always drag a bush strip</u>. In other words, slow it down and take a good, low level look before committing to land. Be sure to let your passengers know what you're doing. Just because you landed there yesterday doesn't mean you'll make it today. In the true Alaska wilderness, you are 911. Always be prepared to survive - on your own!

In the Alaskan Bush,

Yesterday Does Not Necessarily Equal Today.

Pilots. Learn from the experience of others before you go to Alaska.

Read a lot!

Chapter Nine

BREAK THE CHAIN NOW!

The late 1980's produced a lot of extreme weather where precipitation was measured in feet, not inches. That combined with volcanic activity literally created havoc throughout Alaska.

The following traces the path of a fatal Piper Navajo accident. The result was at the end of a chain of events complicated with the backdrop of weather, darkness, and / or severe terrain.

Break the Chain Now!!!

Sleepmute is a remote village located on the east bank of the Kuskokwim River close to central Alaska.

It was during breakup in the tundra. I'd been to this village a couple of days before in a Cessna 206 with oversized tires.

The runway was very rough with scattered large rocks and numerous muddy potholes with some ice remaining.

I reported the conditions to Flight Service and to the Company.

The customer request was to deliver concrete blocks, concrete, and parts weighing several hundred pounds to the village. I was asked to take a Piper Navajo with that cargo load.

Well, I refused the flight when asked and not only did I refuse the flight, I advised the Company to turn down the anxious customer for a few days until the runway improved. I felt it was too hazardous. They reluctantly agreed.

"Well, they're really good customers but you're probably right. I'll let them know."

The Accident Chain had been broken!

Later in the day, I was dispatched for a flight to McGrath which turned out to be fairly uneventful going out. However, on my return after passing Sparavohn approaching the Alaska Range the mountains became mostly obscured with broken layer tops +/- 12,000 feet. I managed to continue over the top and soon was descending in clear air toward Anchorage. Looking back, I could see tops continuing to build into a clear blue sky. The sun was drifting toward the horizon as I began my descent.

Just before switching radios I heard a disturbing call on our company frequency - "N34F - 46H."

I asked, "46H - 34F Go ahead. What's going on?"

"We've lost radio contact with 23J. They had an engine out over Sparavohn, got it going again, and said they were coming on to Anchorage, then we lost radio contact. Maybe their radios are out."

By this time I had to go over to Anchorage tower.

"See you guys on the ground at Merrill."

"OK, see you there."

As we got together on the ground, the story began to unfold.

Someone had given in to the Sleepmute customer and replaced the 'broken link' in the Chain.

The following is the sequence of events that we know followed by educated speculation as to the final chain of events.

Link #1 The customer called the company for a cargo charter to Sleepmute Village.

Link #2 The village runway was barely suitable for a C-206 with oversize tires as reported by me. It was not suitable for a Navajo loaded with, of all things - concrete. Things can get pretty muddy during Spring Thaw or 'Breakup' as it's called. I refused the flight and suggested that the company turn down that customer. The Company seemed in agreement. <u>The chain was broken.</u>

Link #3 Unknown to me, the company under pressure from the customer assigned the flight later in the day. The only pilot available was our newest pilot, barely a month in Alaska, a good pilot but with most of his experience in the Midwest U.S. areas.
Not being familiar with the village runway, he could and should have refused.

Link #4 The aircraft was loaded, I'm sure to gross, and was launched to Sleepmute.
Upon landing, the aircraft struck a hole in the muddy runway and damaged a wheel and possibly had a light prop strike. The aircraft was stuck in the mud.
The aircraft was eventually unloaded but sat on the runway stranded. The incident wasn't necessarily pilot technique but could have been more about the hidden runway conditions!

Link #5 However, after an hour or so, the company decided to send another Navajo with a mechanic and tools to rescue the first aircraft. As the first aircraft had been cleared from the runway, the rescue aircraft was able to land avoiding the worst areas reported on the runway. The tools were unloaded and the mechanic started to work. The repairs were made, run-ups seemed good and both were ready to leave. The rescue aircraft delivering the mechanic and tools left first single pilot and was soon followed by the damaged Aircraft. It had been decided that the mechanic fly back to Anchorage on the damaged aircraft in case there were any further problems.

(With weather over the Alaska Range a consideration could have been to fly over to Aniak or Bethel for a test flight and further maintenance if needed.)

Link #6 The lead aircraft with one pilot was approximately over the Alaska Range when the second aircraft called, "N46H – 23J, we've got an engine problem… The left engine is running very rough."

"Where are you guys?" the Lead Pilot called.

"Our position is over the Sparavohn VOR," called the damaged aircraft pilot. (Sparavohn is an Air Force Radar Site with a 4,000-foot runway.)

"Is there anything I can do?" called the pilot of the lead aircraft.

"Negative, I believe we have a magneto problem."

After a few moments, "We now have an engine out!"

Trying to get a restart!"

(Time for a landing with weather ahead and plenty of runway below them.) <u>Break the Chain Now!!</u>

However, after several minutes, "OK.........we've got it going again." "We're going to continue on to Anchorage."

"Are you sure you can make it?" Yea, it's running ok now. See you in town."

(Put it on the ground now and let's talk about it! Remember the Alaska Range Mountains ahead were obscured with the tops of the broken layer at least at 12,000 feet. If they were to lose the engine at or above that altitude, at best single engine climb, they would be descending at 300 to possibly 500 FPM!)

The chain continued unbroken although there were numerous opportunities to do so. "It's running OK now." was their last communication heard.

As the lead aircraft pilot approached Anchorage, he again tried to contact the damaged aircraft supposedly in trail. Receiving nothing but silence, he notified the company.

Knowing the approximate track, the company planned a search and all available in the company, including myself, participated. The FAA and NTSB were notified.

As darkness set in, we along with Search and Rescue had to abandon the search.

All that remained was educated speculation and worry.

The aircraft was found the next day thanks to military radar tracking records. The radar track showed the aircraft over the Alaska Range traveling a straight line to Anchorage, 13,000 feet, speed 160 knots. Suddenly the airspeed dropped to 100 knots, the aircraft began a descent and promptly made a 90-degree left turn. (This to me indicates an engine out and a turn toward a possible escape route.) The descent continued until disappearing off radar around 11,000 feet.

Early the next morning Alaskan Search and Rescue were following the radar track given by the military and were soon over the crash site. They reported the aircraft seemingly intact, sitting on a glacier. It appeared and was reported that the nose baggage doors were open and there was survival gear near by the front of the aircraft.

Some were excited and all of us were cautiously relieved to hear the news thinking that they were probably OK and had remained in the aircraft to keep warm.

I left with management personnel shortly thereafter to fly up and survey the crash site. We managed to circle approximately 2,000 ft. above and looked intensely for tracks or any sign of life. Some aboard our aircraft were related to the mechanic so tensions were high. We noticed no movement or tracks leading from the aircraft.

We'd circled for some time and were made aware a S.A.R. Helicopter was approaching. We moved away and continued to circle nearby.

However, shortly after the helicopter landed, everyone knew the story was over. Both the Pilot and the Mechanic were killed instantly due to a flat impact on the glacier. The aircraft appeared to be undamaged but was instead flattened.

Both were sitting in their seats with belts on.

It was a tough flight going home to Anchorage.

Like several others scattered through the Alaska Range, the aircraft remains a part of the glacier to this day.

My feeling is that they did indeed lose the bad engine again, this time at 13,000 feet over a broken to possibly overcast mountain range. The mountains underneath had been occasionally visible to me looking straight down through the clouds.

As mentioned earlier there's a subtle thing I've observed when flying in mountains with glaciated areas. On occasion, when the sun gets to a low angle, with sunlight filtering through the mountains and underneath the clouds, the glaciers catch direct sunlight and become illuminated, bright almost like a sunny opening in the mountains.

I believe they were descending through this broken layer with full power on the good engine, saw the brightness, and headed for it. At the last few seconds, they realized their mistake, tried to pull out, but contacted in a high-speed stall condition. It was a severe loss for the Company and for the Family and a sad ending for two great guys.

Always be Aware of small decisions that may become Links in an Accident Chain!

Remember, even with a solid twin engine aircraft be sure to check your single engine performance. If you cannot maintain a course due to terrain on one engine at your current weight best to work out an alternative route for your 'Out'.

Also, if your aircraft manual shows good single engine performance at your planned altitude be sure to reduce that performance at least 1 or 2% for every year since new. Also consider additional drag induced by skin damage or prop leading edge damage, worn and faded paint and any new antennas installed.

Chapter Ten

TEN GOLDEN RULES FOR STAYING ALIVE

To summarize a lot of what has appeared in this book I've developed 10 Golden Rules for surviving in Alaska.

One of these rules may simply save your life someday.

GOLDEN RULE 1

REMEMBER - OXYGEN! (NOT THE O2 KIND.)

Just as the briefing goes on the airlines – Place the mask on yourself, breathe normally, and then help others! If you go under you can't help anyone.

A Captain's Decision –'Living' Decisions

On occasion I wake up with a remorseful thought concerning decisions made when working as a Medevac pilot. Yes, I wake up somewhat remorseful, But, I Wake Up.

There are no remorseful thoughts about any other actions taken as a charter or commuter pilot in situations in Alaska such as, "Sir, you'll have to leave your cooler of Salmon here." Donate it to the nearest village, etc. or "Sorry, we can't pick you up today but possibly tomorrow afternoon if the weather cooperates." etc.

Be aware however, there may be a circumstance in Alaska where you have to make a life or death decision concerning others.

For example,

We were called out around 2:00 AM to fly to one of the northern villages.

It was winter and extremely cold with low ceilings and precipitation. The village runway was + /- 3,000 feet, gravel with no lights.

There were three burn victims from an explosion and fire in their home, a common malady in the bush. They needed attention immediately.

Our Conquest II was the only Medevac aircraft available.

As my co-pilot Tom arrived, we immediately sped into our individual preflight duties. Familiar with the field we both were somewhat skeptical about getting in.

Tom completed the preflight and helped the nurses load their gear and get set up.

However, the more I investigated conditions, the less likely it seemed we could get in and out of there safely. The only way to get below the ceiling was to shoot an approach at the closest IFR airport and scud run to the village.

The Chief of the Village said he thought they could get their fire pots lined up along the sides and at the very least they could shine their headlights alongside and down the runway.

The Conquest II has the capability to land and takeoff in that short distance however with the current conditions there's no margin for safety. The runway condition was another unknown factor. After some discussion, we both agreed on a safer alternative.

The Medevac pilot's First Duty is to see to the safety of his Crew and Flight Nurses. I had a copilot and two nurses for this mission.

Regretfully too many of these crews die while on rescue missions.

As Captain on this flight, I made the decision to land at the nearest IFR airport and have the patients transport by ground to meet us there. Even that turned out to be a tight approach with ice and low ceilings.

Regretfully it took the village very basic ambulance almost two hours to get to us. The critical patients had some care enroute but were in very bad shape.

The nurses went to work immediately preparing them for transport.

In those critical situations the flight crew could easily catch criticism from some but we generally didn't from our nurses. Most were experienced and aware of the hazardous conditions involved.

As had happened many times before Tom and I engaged in assisting the nurses to stabilize our patients and shortly we had three critical patients aboard and departed for Anchorage.

The nurses worked fervently with the patients during the flight. However, quietly one nurse slipped forward and whispered that the one closest behind my seat probably would not make it.

Both of us pilots looked at each other but said nothing. We were doing all we could to make maximum speed.

Our job was to deliver seven folks to Anchorage with three into the waiting hands of the Anchorage Paramedics and the Providence Burn ward.

We were about 30 minutes out when I felt something bump my armrest. Tom looked at me then pointed behind me. I turned in my seat and at that instance saw an arm drop toward the cabin floor. The nurse came forward, placed his arm back across his chest, checked the patient then leaned forward and quietly whispered that he was deceased.

Waves of nausea gripped me for a few moments.

I soon recovered but mentally questioned what had happened.

I mentally asked myself, "Had I attempted a landing at the village – was I wrong about conditions – What if... What if...

Tom I guess saw my mental thoughts and said quietly through my headset, "It was the right decision."

We landed shortly thereafter and assisted in getting all three onto gurneys and into the waiting ambulances.

After some discussion during our post flight duties, Tom and I agreed that we had made the right decision. There were simply too many unknowns.

On a cold dark miserable Alaskan night, we had saved two lives and delivered four crewmembers safely back to Anchorage.

This was my first one lost. With more than 300 Medevac missions through the years, that wasn't the only one I would lose. All I'm saying is

<u>**Oxygen! -**</u>
Stay alive to save others.

GOLDEN RULE 2

DECISION MAKING RULE

Resist external pressures

OK You're a million miles from nowhere. You as Pilot in Command are the Captain of your Ship! You make the Decisions.

In that process forget Passenger, Company, Boss, Financial, Client or Get-Home Pressures. None of these should weigh in to your decision to go or not go, to land or not land, to fuel or not take on fuel.

None of those factors will keep you alive. However, any one of those factors can sure be the end of you and your passengers.

Seems like a no brainer, however possibly hundreds of aircraft have gone down due to a pilot succumbing to one or two of these pressures.

You may disappoint people with your decisions, cause them to change plans, frustrate them to no end. "Gonna' miss my connecting flight!"

Sometimes making the right decision can cost you a good client or possibly your job. There's other clients and other jobs.

Here's an example from my own experience.

The mission was to pick up <u>three</u> fishermen from a somewhat remote strip.

I had just landed in light rain with a strong cross wind on a short gravel runway with occasional large rocks and holes.

As I opened the cabin door of my Cessna 402 I observed <u>five</u> <u>big guys</u>, their Alaska gear plus five coolers of salmon.

The operational factors plus trees on both ends told me I did not need to attempt a takeoff with that load.

As I approached, I could see pride written all over their faces. They were taking pictures, talking about how their family and friends are really going to love these wonderful fish.

After a short greeting they were ready to throw everything on board and get going out of this horrible cold rain.

I asked them to hold up just a minute, climbed back aboard and worked out my weight and balance. As I looked at my max weight to meet my takeoff requirements, I knew for sure that flying that load out wasn't going to happen.

"What do you mean we can't take three of our coolers?" "Look there's plenty of room for them."

"I spent a lot of money on this fishing trip." On and on…

Another comment, "We flew out of here OK last year!"

Beware – it's usually one ignorant loud voice that's trying to lead everyone else into Heaven's gate a little early.

Pilots have acquiesced and attempted such ridiculous feats based on a loud customer claiming they had done it before. Take my advice, don't die today. Somebody gets to donate fish and coolers to the local native population, the lodge, or to the bears.

I offered to make another trip or to ferry 2 or 3 smaller loads to a better and longer runway somewhere if I could get someone's credit card up front.

The answer after a bit– "donate the fish to the village".

After that takeoff the chatter subsided and Guess what? We all arrived healthy and alive back in Anchorage.

As professional pilots we're trained to make our decisions based on operational factors such as weather, equipment, pilot readiness and our experience level and to operate within legal parameters.

Your decisions in Bush Operations have to be based on those same Operational, Legal, and Personal Limitations!

Evaluating Risk Factors is a key part of flying in Alaska and from a passenger's viewpoint, you might want to thank the pilot for being conservative in his decision making and not complain. However it's OK to ask questions and be an active participant in a risk evaluation discussion. Speak up if you feel a questionable decision isn't safe.

If, after discussing the aspects you are still not satisfied with the plan, you don't have to go along with it! Go home, or remain where you are. Wait another day or find another company.

A rather humorous accident, at least to the folks watching the feat. Kenai Peninsula – calm and clear day. A heavily loaded Cessna 206 on floats departing from a small lake made the rounds to get the water good and agitated and without pausing made his takeoff attempt. Regretfully he ran out of water a micro second before his floats had cleared. The floats stopped at the shoreline, the aircraft and people continued on Terra Firma in a beautiful full throttle 206 sled. Eventually about 10 seconds later the pilot knew he had a problem as it was taking full throttle to taxi back down to the lake. (That part is a joke. The accident was not.) Everyone amazingly walked away from that one.

The witnesses watching the event thought it was the most spectacular way of removing floats they'd ever seen. Oh yeah, Always wear your shoulder harness in Alaska (or anywhere actually) as it may keep your face from becoming a part of the instrument panel.

GOLDEN RULE 3

ALWAYS LEAVE YOURSELF AN 'OUT'

This is a basic rule and generally speaks for itself.

All instructors should be identifying for their students the 'Outs' available to meet every possible abnormal or emergency operation during their early days of training.

For instance, on climb out from your airport, what would you do if you lose an engine – Fly straight ahead and land in the trees? Or turn left 20 degrees and land in the spacious field?

I usually took a little longer in soloing my students just to ensure for the pattern regime they knew how to handle every emergency and knew every possible out available to them.

In that regard, I observed a U-Tube video the other day with a very confident and seemingly knowledgeable instructor demonstrating to his new student what to listen for right after takeoff? He lifted the nose until he got a solid stall warning horn... On Takeoff! At about 200 feet. I guess he missed the wind shear chapter as well as never dreamed he could have an engine barf right at that moment. There's a reason for the 1500 Foot rule folks and that is to Leave Yourself an 'Out'. You cannot use the altitude above you when falling.

They survived thus the video. However, the next step in the chain is that the student with his new license shows this to his girlfriend or three buddies on a humid day with thunderstorms in the vicinity - a setup for disaster.

Leaving yourself an out may simply be height above Terra Firma when performing maneuvers. An inadvertent stall spin low to the ground can ruin a good day of flying.

Also, always respect your IFR minimums. They're there for a reason.

However, in Alaska especially I realize there are a lot of one-way airports whereas you're landing against a mountainside etc. That possibly is the only exception once you're committed.

Having been into and out of some of the most dramatic one-way airstrips in Alaska I learned to make a sound plan for escape at different distances. Once you're down below your escape routes and committed, you're only out may be to focus on your approach and landing and especially focus on your airspeed to control your landing distance.

GOLDEN RULE 4

PLAN AHEAD FOR DIFFERENT SCENARIOS

Fly like a Professional.

Don't be surprised when something goes wrong. Plan for those scenarios and be quite surprised when everything goes as planned.

As mentioned earlier consider the winds aloft above and below your planned altitude especially in mountainous terrain. Consider them in relation to what you would do with an engine out or other emergency situation or having to climb to get over icing in unexpected cloud tops.

So you're only flying at 5,000 feet and nowhere near the peaks of the mountains off to the east and not really concerned about the winds at 10,000 and 12,000.

Well... If the peaks are parallel to your course of flight and perpendicular to the wind direction at those peaks you could encounter some severe rotor clouds, mountain waves and other forms of clear air turbulence.

One of the hardest jolts I've gotten into was flying a Seneca from Anchorage to Palmer on a nice clear day. Winds at the surface were light. I was fairly new to the area, winds aloft for 3 and 6 thousand were forecast 15 knots and out of the Northeast.

As I flew approximately past Birchwood, I encountered gut wrenching up and down drafts, hit my head and promptly dropped my seat and tightened my belt. The next jolt cracked one of the rear windows. Flying attitude and a low power setting I eventually got clear.

Know your aircraft's power settings for level, climb, and descent scenarios. You may not be able to depend on your airspeed indicator or other static instruments in this situation.

The turbulence I encountered was from high wind turbulence spilling off the Chugach mountain range, a phenomenon I later learned was fairly common in the Anchorage area.

Think 'What ifs' such as flying home multi-engine with an engine caged. Terrain is 10,000 along the route. Look at altitudes required, possible landing strips and weather along your planned route. What's the temperature at your planned altitude and weather possibilities such as Ice?

Alright, it's – 58 at 12,000 feet. Heater failure? Can you and your passengers make it should that happen? Got any survival gear aboard.

It's – 45 and you'll be on the ground 25 minutes. Ever had an oleo strut expire on the ground at a remote strip. Can't stay... You'll have to drag the gear all the way home. Do you have enough fuel aboard to get there in that case?

Just Think... What ifs?

GOLDEN RULE 5

*FOLLOW COMMON AND SPECIFIC RULES AND
PROCEDURES EVEN WHEN IN THE WILDERNESS*

*Most airports in Alaska are non-controlled. Use caution,
be vigilant, communicate, and utilize proper entry and
departure procedures even if you think you're the only
aircraft in the area.*

In that regard, never taxi into position and hold at a non-controlled airport. Sitting with your back to the final approach corridor waiting for an aircraft to clear or to complete a takeoff run is not a good practice. Sure you observed no one on final just before you pulled out. However... What about the hard to see Cessna 310 approaching on a straight in Final? What if he had lost radios or switched to the wrong frequency when handed off by approach. What if the fellow downwind abeam had an engine failure and did not see you as he was watching the aircraft on takeoff roll, then in a panic state forgot to announce his intention to land – while you're sitting there blind to the final approach corridor.

Also be ready for another pilot to make an illegal and unthinkable move and enter your flight path on takeoff or landing. I had such an experience and near miss with a brightly colored 'no-rad' bi-wing sport plane.

Although announcing my positions for landing in the left traffic pattern, on short final the aircraft pulled onto the runway right in front of me. I was in a Cessna 402B at approach speed with gear and full flaps.

I powered up and moved to the right at low level, announced my 'go around' and began cleaning my aircraft while keeping the aircraft in sight. Suddenly, the aircraft went to a right oblique climbing turn right in front of my windshield!

I had no choice but to dive toward the runway in a hard left turn passing underneath the aircraft!

He passed above me, seemingly oblivious that I was there!

Stay on the Defensive at all times.

GOLDEN RULE 6

DO NOT SCUD RUN AS A NORMAL PRACTICE

It will eventually get you.

One of my best students amazingly committed to his Private, Commercial, and Multi-Engine Training was a 709 Ride Candidate who under Part 135 landed his perfectly good Cessna 207 with six aboard, yes in the flat tundra. It seems that the FAA frowned upon such doings.

He explained to me he'd been between the villages many times at that altitude feeling his way back and forth.

However this one time... perhaps it was indeed colder than most days whereas his aircraft's actual altitude was lower than indicated.

Regardless, he was totally surprised when he contacted Terra Firma. White out, Gray out, Flat Light - it doesn't matter. Scud running as a normal practice is not a good plan.

The case is that some weather phenomenon has a way of bending light rays and obscuring or disguising familiar terrain features.

One of our 402's came back from a mail run with limbs from a treetop stuck in the wheel wells. That pilot survived his scud running incident, learned his lesson and vowed to never try it again.

It's not just us GA pilots that sometimes are guilty. A Mark Air Boeing 737 on a deadhead leg, landed 2 miles short of the destination runway after getting a 'lowest descent vector' in a nearby valley, then attempted to scud run to the airport.

Both these incidents were in familiar territory along a repeated route.

Scud Run Roulette is Not a good plan for a long flight career or for a long life for that matter.

GOLDEN RULE 7

RESOURCE MANAGEMENT

Use all information and resources available to you.

As mentioned earlier, yes, even to make a run over the Knik Arm Channel check low level wind direction and velocity.

You always want to talk to other pilots who may have experience in your planned destination area.

Cross Check Instruments.

111

If flying a two-pilot crew, remember there's no place for exaggerated Egos in the cockpit.

Plan to take a Crew Resource Management class which also includes Single Pilot Resource management.

Single Pilot Resource Management may include help from a passenger or passengers.

Here's such an incident...

Alaskan Nights are very dark so always be prepared for a Power Failure.

This incident occurred on takeoff on a very dark and dreary night with 1,000 overcast and about 2 miles visibility.

I'd just gotten into the air when just prior to 'Gear Up' everything went dark. No panel lights and all instruments were dark. No gear lights, no cabin lights.

I had my hand on the gear switch but caught myself before cycling and left the gear in place.

I pulled the flashlight to see my instruments and began a right turn back around to the airport. All that is somewhat of a challenge to say the least. Luckily I had a female passenger in the right seat who offered and courageously assisted me by holding the flashlight on the instruments.

It was dark, very dark. She also helped me run through the emergency checklists as I had my hands full of airplane. Nothing worked. I primarily focused on simply flying the aircraft and maintaining contact with the runway.

I flew a standard pattern and looked to the tower for landing clearance. On the downwind I looked and observed no other aircraft on final. I continued around on a modified base leg. Now the runway was fully illuminated and yes indeed, a bright green light was now emitting from the tower. I suspected they saw my lights disappear. With this steady handed passenger's assistance, we were almost home. I think her name was Julie.

We were not out of the woods yet with no landing lights and especially no gear lights. I luckily hadn't cycled the gear after takeoff so I reasoned they were still down and locked. However, still a little disconcerting.

I planned to be as smooth as possible and be prepared for the worst.

Squeaking the Mains on - Normal touchdown, now the nose wheel, yes.... Normal.

Flashing Green was now coming from the tower and I taxied to the gate.

Hey guys, I've run into a lot of strong and courageous women in Alaska. I've actually seen it most of my life, especially with the flight nurses and also in combat situations in Vietnam. When the chips are down, they'll do what they have to do, even after thinking it over. This fine lady that helped me out was definitely one of those women. Thanks Julie. You were awesome!

GOLDEN RULE 8

FLY – NAVIGATE – COMMUNICATE

This is your order of Priorities. You've heard that time and time again. Keep these in order and you have a much better chance of surviving in this business.

FLY!   AIRSPEED, AIRSPEED, AIRSPEED!!!

For instance, one of my questions about crashes where pilots die usually with someone else aboard is "Why were they talking to ATC instead of getting themselves out of the situation".

A horrid example is that of a pilot and his wife aboard a Cherokee Six on fire at 2,000 feet and calling for help on the radio. They eventually crashed – Two Fatals.

PUT THE AIRCRAFT ON THE GROUND NOW! From that altitude that can happen in less than 30 seconds!

Dive in a slip, fly any altitude, any configuration, any airspeed required to Position Yourself on Short - Short Final with full drag configuration if possible. Get to proper landing speed even if it's a crash landing. Get clear of the aircraft. Deal with the rest later.

Always Fly First. Maintain control of your aircraft.

ATC communications are excellent 99.9 % of the time where things are handled well and safely.

However, knowing exactly where you are at all times should become a natural trait.

Trust controllers to a point, a point where you feel things might not be as they should. Remember it's ok to question an assigned runway, altitude or vector or any instruction if you feel there's a problem or better option.

'Flying off their assigned screen on a busy day' can cause such a problem. I've been on a vector more than once and with no heading changes from ATC saw (VFR conditions) or knew I was being vectored into high terrain.   On one particular day in California in an IFR on top condition, I continued on an assigned vector, arrived and called in close to the mountain side just to make a point. They do get busy so know where you are at all times. Be aware of improper clearances!

Know where you are at all times.

Legal may not equate to safe.

I'm sure you've heard this one. "If a pilot makes a critical mistake, the Pilot dies. If the Controller makes a critical mistake, the Pilot dies."

Also Remember, they cannot help you with an onboard fire or damaged aircraft. <u>Take care of it yourself.</u> Get the aircraft on the ground or on the surface of the water!

Just keep that in mind. Only you are responsible for you. Know where you are at All Times!

Lights Out:

Another Incident:

On a cold dark winter's night - sounds ominous doesn't it, I was returning from McGrath with a full load of passengers in a Cessna 402 Single Pilot.

I'd encountered moderate turbulence and high winds enroute due to a fast-moving front. In Alaska, these things simply pop up out of nowhere. Much of the weather encountered in the Lower 48 begins in North West Alaska. We didn't have much warning in those days.

Normally, I'm Mister 'fuel' with lots of reserve. However, tonight, I arrived on minimum fuel due to heavy head winds, turbulence, snow and ice. It was very dark which generally works in one's favor on a minimums approach.

Arriving in the area, I tuned in ATIS for Anchorage.

"Anchorage information foxtrot, ceiling 100 overcast, visibility ½ mile, moderate snow."

As Buck used to say, "OOOOHHHH Boy! Better nail this one."

I had a nice straight in approach situation and picked up the localizer several miles out.

Due to icing reported and turbulence, I decided to hand fly the aircraft to avoid any surprises or a sudden autopilot disconnect. I finished my descent check and before landing checklists.

I was totally focused. "Needles centered. On Glideslope. Speed checks. Flaps approach. Approaching Glide Slope, Gear Down. On Speed, Needles centered, descent rate normal, on Glideslope, 500 feet, On speed, Needles centered, On Glideslope, 300 feet. Needles centered, on glideslope, 100 feet, quick glance, needles centered, 50 feet above minimums, needles centered, Decision Height, Power up, Pitch up, establish climb. No lights anywhere!

"Dang! I know it should be there." In my initial climb a glow from my left caught my attention. Glancing quickly, I could see a glow from the terminal area and Anchorage, but below there was no runway lighting of any kind.

On the missed, I called tower.

"Anchorage tower, Twin Cessna 57J on the missed approach."

"Roger, 57J, contact Approach.

"Can you check the runway lights? They seem to be off."

"Standby. Fifteen seconds went by.

"Lights are on. 57J contact approach."

I wasn't sure what that meant. No time for discussion here. Possibly someone had thrown a wrong switch somewhere. As I went back to approach control, I was in moderate snow, icing, darkness and still somewhat concerned about lighting.

This had to be my last approach here. Elmendorf was calling in the back of my mind. Those controllers were pretty darn good. I'd worked with all my instrument students in the past shooting GCA approaches to minimums there.

Fuel was quickly becoming more of a problem now as I began eating into my reserves. Everything in the basin was down to 100 feet and ½ mile or less. However, I felt somewhat confident knowing I could probably put it on the centerline zero - zero if I had to. We had practiced that on occasion when flying with two pilots.

"Anchorage Approach, 57J is ready to execute another ILS approach to Anchorage."

Carrying ice, I knew I had to get this bird on the ground and soon. I cycled the boots once more. Following vectors back to final I was cleared again for the approach.

Again, I completed all before landing checks and went totally focused, centering every needle and making every detail perfect. About 400 Feet and halfway down the glideslope the clouds began getting brighter. At 300 feet I began picking up the approach lights now a mile out. What do you know - There's the runway, all bright and everything!

Other than "Cleared to land. "Taxi to parking," nothing else was said by the tower and I didn't complain. I was just glad to be home.

Maintenance issue? Controller mistake? We'll never know.

GOLDEN RULE 9

BE PREPARED TO SURVIVE ON YOUR OWN.

If you're departing for a destination outside of the immediate area of any of the cities in Alaska or in any other mountainous state, be ready to survive. A Human 'Bean' is quite low on the natural food chain.

This means having a means to last several days with no outside help.

On <u>every</u> flight carry with you at least some basic items to help you last a few days.

Dress appropriately or have available clothing, boots, gloves and waterproof gear.

If you're simply up and down flight instructing it's wise to keep a few items in your flight bag as well. One is a good mosquito net as there are some areas where the mosquitos and black flies will literally eat you alive. Another is a couple of large heavy duty rolled up Black Trash Bags with a couple of large and small bungies. Simply cut small arm holes and a hole for your head and slip over your clothing and secure with a bungie around your waist. A couple of small ones with bungies can keep your feet dry as well. This simple tactic for survival will help preserve body heat and keep you dry. Hypothermia is not a joke!

Have along some type of safe fire starter. How about a small bag or two of Fritos – excellent fuel to establish a good camp fire. Just strike a match to a pile and experiment yourself. Don't use them all at once as about 10 chips will burn for 5 minutes. You can eat the other 45. Not bad to get a few carbos and a little grease in you. They take up very little space and weigh nothing.

On flights outside the area or in any mountainous country I recommend complying with the published survival gear requirement and carrying a good survival Weapon.

GOLDEN RULE 10

ALWAYS BE WHERE YOU ARE.

Have PRESCENCE OF MIND during your Pilot duties.

Pilots need to have a solid presence of mind on all phases of flight especially during critical regimes of flight. However,

For instance – While hurriedly moving automatically through your preflight, someone watching asks you a question. Best to stop what you're doing, answer the question, and then resume your preflight focus. Talking and moving through your preflight may leave a section blank in your memory or possibly cause you to forget something.

"Did I replace the oil cap securely? Did I actually check it?"

Ever have that gnawing feeling? If so, best to get out the ladder and check it again.

Did I ensure the nose baggage door was locked? Better check it.

Rushing along can also cause you to skip a checklist item and may very well begin an accident chain. Especially have presence of mind about your aircraft's condition or configuration of critical items like your Flap and Fuel Selector settings for takeoffs and landings.

Case: A Final Accident Chain...

This accident followed a chain of events in that regard concerning a Cessna 402 short ferry flight from Anchorage

International to Merrill Field with marginal night VFR weather.

Link #1

On landing at Anchorage, the pilot had, with possible 'Get Home ITIS', hurried through or ignored his checklist for landing and left his fuel position levers in the Aux position. 'Takeoff and Land on Main Tanks only' is on the checklist and placarded adjacent to the fuel selector.

Link #2

After a normal landing and taxi, he quickly dropped his passengers off and again obviously skipped through his Checklist a second time missing 'Takeoff and land on Main Tanks only".

Link #3

Took off without incident, then began his descending turn toward Merrill. At only three miles from touchdown, lost an engine, Reported it to ATC as he attempted to switch tanks on the dead engine. Before the first engine caught up, he lost the other engine due to the same problem and with two engines out had no time to do anything else but land.

From there he obviously lined up on a dark area which was more or less an empty field. He extended the gear and flaps, however...

Link #4

Estimated at about 300 feet, the first engine lost, caught up and went to full throttle creating a VMC rollover and spin. Both the pilot and his one passenger aboard were killed.

(Emergency Engine - Out Landing Checklist was not followed. ie 'Mixtures to Idle Cutoff.')

(I worked with the NTSB on this crash whereas we examined the site then flew simulations with the same model aircraft measuring various angles of attack with one engine operating solely on the auxiliary tank. In our case the engine continued to run even at steep descent angles. There were no obvious results in our tests however the exact conditions and pilot controls at the time of the engine out incident were unknown.)

The next item tends to fall somewhere between distractions and common sense. That is when a Businessman, Doctor or other Professional has the finances to afford a nice high-performance aircraft for his travels. I've flown with and trained several.

When they check in with some aircraft salesmen whose theory is, "You might as well buy and train in the aircraft you want to be traveling in." and they follow the lead, they start out with a Handicap. I think that many accidents involving those folks are caused by gaps in training and lack of stick and rudder skills and experience as an airman in general.

I say to those buying an aircraft for personal travel, Get some training in various related aircraft to the one you intend to purchase. Work your way through for instance several Cessna Singles and twins before you climb into a Cessna Citation Mustang!

Also, after you've completed your training for the aircraft, at least attain additional training in other aircraft and take other courses such as Mountain Flying or Aerobatic training.

Another very important additional safety precaution for the new aircraft owner is to have an instructor or safety pilot with high time in the right seat especially in marginal weather or into unfamiliar airports or terrain.

Another Phenomenon I discovered flying right seat as an Instructor or Safety Pilot with professionals, whether businessmen, political types, contractors or doctors is that they can 'Leave' the cockpit mentally. I've found that for instance a businessman is speaking at a meeting shortly after arrival or is a contractor submitting a bid by noon, etc., that many times 20 - 30 minutes out from landing they can leave the cockpit mentally and if alone could end up a statistic.

It's not just those folks who can leave the cockpit a little early. Pilots including professionals can be out there as well.

Always 'Be Where You Are!

Here's another item to consider that can lead us any of us into oblivion.

How about the devices we carry today?

Don't let your 'devices' interrupt your process during any phase of flight.

Just because the general public is 'dumbing and numbing' due to all their devices doesn't mean we as pilots have to succumb to it.

Dumbing and Numbing

'This picture will probably evoke the reality of what's happening to the general public.

Shortly after boarding as a passenger for a recent flight sitting about mid-way back and in an aisle seat, I observed that all the window shades were down on the aircraft including my row. It was mid-morning!

The aircraft was a Boeing 757, a rather large aircraft departing on a 3 ½ hour flight. I had a good view of the cabin both forward and aft.

My first thought was that the aircraft had returned from a late-night trip and they simply had not opened any of the shades.

However, we pushed back and began a rather long taxi for takeoff and not one person raised a shade to look outside the aircraft.

To my amazement, 90 % had some sort of device on their lap or in their hands. No one was talking.

After 20 minutes, we were pressed against our seats as the enormous thrust of the engines sounded. Shortly we were obviously airborne as the vibration of the wheels on the runway ended.

Now I'm both dumbfounded and quite uncomfortable being in a giant tube with a couple of hundred people hurtling through the air low to the ground at 250 mph and accelerating.

As the flight progressed, I attempted to ignore the situation. However, after a couple of hours, I couldn't help but look around and observe the passengers somewhat individually. Who are these people?

There was silence - no communication. All had glowing faces and a blank stare into their devices.

I suddenly realized that their minds were totally occupied and that no one knew where they were or could care less. Now I'm reminded of a sci-fi movie a little while back where all the population was addicted to a translucent light which was quite pleasant right up to the point where they all died after forgetting to eat or drink.

It was a Saturday, not particularly a business day or a business crowd and after three hours of flight the picture had not changed.

What material were they into? Some quick glances while walking the aisle revealed some books but mostly 'Bubblegum' for the brain.

There was no sound or communication, an eerie silence prevailed. While most still stared into their devices, some were sleeping slumped over their glowing computers.

The overall visual impression was of manikins or dummies belted into a test aircraft.

Near the end of our flight, the 'manikins' finally came alive only because they were told to shut off their devices for the landing approach. I suppose we landed as it felt like a landing. We evidently parked, the bell sounded, the door opened and everyone got off.

Was that an extreme example or is that becoming the norm?

I've begun to observe more and more people locked into their devices and totally unaware of their surroundings.

If an alert of a national emergency came over the internet or appeared as a text message that told them to go here or there immediately, would they all go like sheep without a question or thinking about the situation?

Be careful folks. Don't be 'dumbed down' by these devices to the point of not knowing where you are and to the point of losing common sense.

Be Where You Are. Be With Who You Are With.

Yes, utilize the latest technologies but attempt to balance it against the world outside of that realm. Do not become so addicted that you cannot function otherwise and miss out on the reality of your situation.

'ALWAYS BE <u>WHERE YOU ARE</u>.'

It's very important especially when piloting an aircraft! Don't get locked into any device and forget to look outside.

Fly your aircraft. Be Vigilant.

EPILOGUE

Within this book I realize there's a lot of negative displayed in a somewhat pragmatic sense. It hasn't been easy remembering the deceased as most were friends, however I hope their stories have shed light on some things to watch out for anytime, especially in Alaska. There, a mistake or incident, even a small one can get you killed.

However, I've got to say that out of all my flying career, including jets, my Alaska Time is the most memorable. The comradeship with other pilots, mechanics, and all supporting personnel as well as most passengers were over the top special. The challenges are there daily. The rewards are there as well.

I say if it's in your blood... Go do it. You won't be disappointed. However, build some time in the Lower 48 prior to heading north as Alaska is not a good place to build time as a new pilot.

Blue Skies

Good Flights!

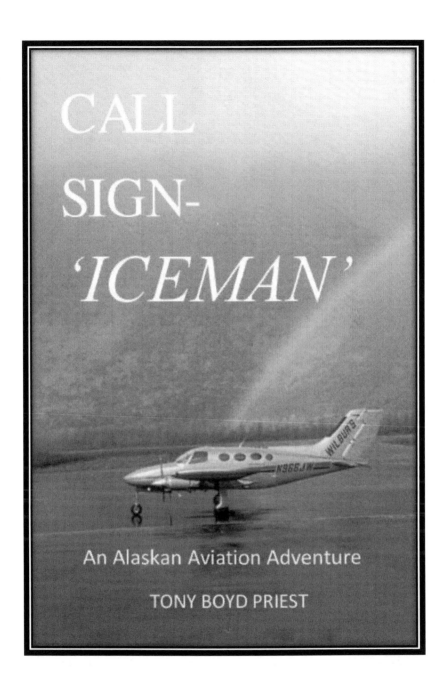

CALL
SIGN-
'ICEMAN'

An Alaskan Aviation Adventure

TONY BOYD PRIEST

ONCE A WARRIOR

Captain Thomas Price

MISSION – ALASKA

TONY BOYD PRIEST

CALL SIGN –
'MOUNTAIN MAN'

Surviving the High Country

TONY BOYD PRIEST

Dear Alaska,

What an awesome privilege it was for me to fly through your beautiful mountain passes, over the vastness of your tundra and to see your pristine rivers, lakes and islands.

I've soaked into my soul the canvas of the soft pastel colors of your skies touting the complete spectrum of the colors of the rainbow.

I've sailed along past your majestic, snowcapped mountains and seen a thousand of your beautiful sunrises and sunsets of yellows, gold's and reds, sometimes at the hour of midnight.

I've sailed over your deep, aqua blue, sometimes emerald green waters strewn with the brilliant whiteness of the ice. Your crystal clear rivers, sometimes placid, were often raging as they weaved through your pristine wilderness.

I've seen firsthand the unstoppable forces of nature, humbling even the strongest and heartiest of souls.

I've watched as millions of sea birds all took flight at the same time, changing the colors of the landscape from green and blue to white.

I've shared with my kindred Alaskan people, sadness and loss, but also happiness and good cheer.

Thank You Alaska for sharing your Great Land, your wonderful people, your mystery and your challenge.

Thank You God, for allowing me to be there and to become an integral part of your beautiful Creation. Amen.

Tony Boyd Priest
June 28, 1990

130

Made in the USA
Columbia, SC
09 October 2024

44029392R00078